D0198135

Kate Needham

Illustrated by Ann Johns

Designed by Kathy Ward

Language consultants: Zina Rahouadj and Pascal Varejka

Edited by Rachel Firth
Series editor: Sue Meredith

Contents

About the dictionary

This dictionary lists up-to-date words you need to get around in France. If the word you want is missing, try to think of a different one that you could use instead. In the English to French list (pages 4-43), illustrations with labels provide lots of extra words. Below are some tips on using the dictionary.

A typical entry in the English to French list looks like this:

This is the word you looked up.

This is the French translation.

red rouge *rooj*

This is the French pronunciation hint. Read it as if it were an English word and you will be close to the French.

"**or**" introduces an extra French translation. Words in brackets after "or" hint at the difference in meaning:

ball la balle *bal,* **or (large)** le ballon *ba-lon*

le/la Most French nouns (see page 44) are masculine or feminine. So that you know which each is, they are listed with the French for "the" - usually le for masculine nouns and la for feminine nouns. Nouns that can be either are listed with le/la:

cinema le cinéma *see-naima*
station la gare *gar*
tourist le/la touriste *tooreest*

[m] stands for masculine
[f] stands for feminine

For nouns that begin with a vowel (or sometimes h), "the" is l'; for plural nouns it is les. So that you know if these are masculine or feminine, they are followed by [m] or [f] - or [m/f] if they can be either.

(e) Most French adjectives, and a few nouns, have two forms: masculine and feminine. The feminine is often made by adding an e (or another letter and e) to the masculine. Often both forms are said the same way. In this case, you will see the masculine, a bracket showing the letters you add for the feminine, and then the pronunciation:

pretty joli(e) *jolee*

f: The extra letters can make the feminine sound different from the masculine. If so, you will see f: with a second pronunciation:

grey gris(e) *gree* f: *greez*

If the feminine word is very different, you will see f: followed by the feminine word spelled out in full, and its pronunciation:

fresh frais frai f: fraîche *fraish*

pl: introduces any unusual plural you need to know about:

eye l'oeil [m] *uh-yuh* pl: les yeux *yuh*

***** indicates that words are familiar or mild slang, and are best avoided in formal situations:

chaos la pagaille* *pag-eye*

****** indicates words that are very familiar or slangy, or that would be offensive if used in the wrong situation. It is safest to avoid them altogether or at least use them only with friends of your own age:

boring chiant/chiante** *shee-on/shee-ont*

Verbs (see page 44) are listed in the infinitive form, e.g. "to eat", but you will find them listed under "e" for eat, "w" for walk etc.

Here are some useful, ready-made phrases you may need:

I'd like...
Je voudrais
juh voodrai

Could I have...?
Je pourrais avoir...?
juh pooraiz-avwar

Where is...?
Où est?
oo ai...

What's this?
Qu'est-ce que c'est?
kess-kuh sai

I don't understand.
Je ne comprends pas.
je nuh kompron pa

Leave me alone!
Laissez-moi tranquille!
lessai-mwa tronkeel

How much is it?
C'est combien?
sai kombee-an

I'm very sorry.
Je suis désolé(e).
juh swee daizolai

Do you speak English?
Parlez-vous anglais?
parlai-voo onglai

A little slower, please.
Un peu plus lentement, s'il vous plaît.
un puh plew lontmon seel voo plai

Can you write it down for me?
Vous pouvez me l'écrire?
voo vouvai muh laikreer

What's that called in French?
Comment ça s'appelle en français?
kommon sa sappell on fronssai

Could you say that again, please?
Vous pourriez répéter, s'il vous plaît?
voo pooree-ai raipaitai seel voo plai

Could you tell me where the toilet is?
Les toilettes, s'il vous plaît?
lai twalett seel voo plai

Numbers

0 zero *zairo*
1 un(e) *un f: ewnn*
2 deux *duh*
3 trois *trwa*
4 quatre *katr*
5 cinq *sank*
6 six *seess*
7 sept *sett*
8 huit *weet*
9 neuf *nurf*
10 dix *deess*
11 onze *onz*
12 douze *dooz*
13 treize *traiz*
14 quatorze *katorze*
15 quinze *kanz*
16 seize *saiz*
17 dix-sept *dee-sett*
18 dix-huit *deez-weet*
19 dix-neuf *deez-nurf*
20 vingt *van*
21 vingt et un *van-tai-un*
22 vingt-deux *vant-duh*
30 trente *tront*
40 quarante *karont*
50 cinquante *sankont*
60 soixante *swassont*
70 soixante-dix *swassont deess*
71 soixante et onze *swassont-ai-onz*
72 soixante-douze *swassont-dooz*
80 quatre-vingts *katre van*
81 quatre-vingt-un *katre van un*
90 quatre-vingt-dix *katre van deess*
100 cent *son*
101 cent un *son un*
102 cent deux *son duh*
200 deux cents *duh son*
210 deux cent dix *duh son deess*
300 trois cents *trwa son*
1 000 mille *meel*
1 100 mille cent *meel son*
1 200 mille deux cents *meel duh son*
2 000 deux mille *duh meel*
10 000 dix mille *dee meel*
100 000 cent mille *son meel*
1 000 000 un million *un meel-yon*

In Belgium, Switzerland and some parts of France, 70, 80 and 90 are **septante** *septont*, **huitante** *weetont* and **nonante** *nonnont.*

a, an un *un* f: une *ewnn*
abbey l'abbaye [f]: *ab-ai-ee*
abolish abolir *ab-oll-eer*
about (approximately) environ *onveeron;* **what's it about? (film, book)** de quoi ça parle? *duh kwa sa parl*
above au-dessus de *o-duhssew-duh*
abroad à l'étranger *a-lai-tron-jai*
accent l'accent [m] *akson*
to accept accepter *akseptai*
accident l'accident [m] *akseedon*
accommodation (places to stay) le logement *lojmon*
to ache (or to have a head/ back etc. ache) avoir mal à *avwar mal a* **(see picture)**
to act (theatre) jouer *joo-ai*
actor l'acteur [m] *aktuhr*
actress l'actrice [f] *aktreess*
to add ajouter *ajootai*
address l'adresse [f] *adress*
admire admirer *admeerai*
adopted adoptif *adopteef* f: adoptive *adopteev*
adult l'adulte [m/f] *adewlt*
advantage l'avantage [m] *avontaj;* **to take advantage of** profiter de *profeetai duh*
adventurous aventureux *avon-tewruh* f: aventureuse *avon-tewrurz*
advertisement (in paper) l'annonce [f] *annonss,* **or (at cinema, on TV)** la pub* *pewb;* **classified ads** les petites annonces *puhteet-zannonss*
advice le conseil *konssaiy*
to advise conseiller *konssaiy-ai*
aerobics l'aérobic [f] *a-airobeek*
Africa l'Afrique [f] *afreek*
after après *aprai*
afternoon l'après-midi [m/f] *aprai-meedee*
again de nouveau *duh noovo,* **or** encore *onkor*
against contre *kontr*
age l'âge [m] *aj;* **underage** mineur(e) *mee-nuhr*
aggressive agressif *agg-ress-eef f:* agressive agg-ress-eev
ago il y a *eel-ee-a,* **e.g. ten days ago** il y a dix jours
to agree être d'accord *etr dakor*
aid l'aide [f] *ed*
AIDS le SIDA *seeda*
air l'air [m] *air;* **air-conditioned** air conditionné *air kondeess-yonnai*
airline la compagnie aérienne *kompannee a-airee-yenn*
airmail par avion *par av-yon*
airport l'aéroport [m] *a-airopor*
alarm clock le réveil *rev-aiy*
album l'album [m] *albom*
alcohol l'alcool [m] *alkol*
alcoholic alcoolisé(e) *alkoleezai;* **non-alcoholic** sans alcool *son-zalkol*
all tout(e) *too f: toot,* pl: tous *(too)* f: toutes *toot;*
all right (I agree) d'accord *dakor,* **or (it's OK)** ça va *sa-va*
allergy l'allergie [f] *alairjee*
to allow permettre *pair-metr*
almost presque *pressk*
alone seul(e) *surl*
already déjà *dai-ja*
also aussi *o-see*
alternative (not conventional) original(e) *oreejeennal*
always toujours *toojoor*
amazing (unbelievable) incroyable *ankr-wa-yabl,* **or (great)** génial(e) *jainn-yal*
ambulance l'ambulance [f] *ombewlonss*
America l'Amérique [f] *ammaireek*
American américain(e) *ammaireekan f: ammaireekenn*
amuse amuser *am-oo-zai*
and et *ai*
angry en colère *on kolair*
animal l'animal [m] *annee-mal*

to ache avoir mal à

J'ai mal à la tête.
jai mal a la tett
J'ai mal aux dents.
jai mal o don
J'ai mal à l'oreille.
jai mal a loraiy
J'ai mal au ventre.
jai mal o vontr
J'ai mal aux reins.
jai mal o ran

ankle la cheville *shuh-veey*
to annoy énerver *ainnairvai*, **or** agacer *agassai;* **to get annoyed** s'énerver *sainnairvai*
annoying (slightly) embêtant(e) *ombetton f: ombettont,* **or (very)** énervant(e) *ainnairvon f: ainnairvont*
answer la réponse *raiponss*
to answer répondre *raipondr*
answering machine le répondeur *raiponduhr*
antibiotic l'antibiotique [m] *ontee-beeo-teek*
antiseptic antiseptique *ontee-septeek*
any (as in "do you have any matches?") de *duh* **or** du *dew* **or** de la *duh la* **or** de l' *duhl* **or** des *dai*, **or (as in "any old thing")** n'importe quel(le) *namport kel*
anyone quelqu'un *kelkun,* **or (as in "anyone can do it")** n'importe qui *namport kee* **(see also 'nobody')**
anything quelque chose *kelkuh shoze,* **or (as in "anything will do")** n'importe quoi *namport kwa* **(see also 'nothing')**
anywhere quelque part *kelkuh par,* **or (as in "just anywhere")** n'importe où *nampor-too* **(see also 'nowhere')**
apartment l'appartement (m) appahtuhmon
apple la pomme *pomm* **(see also picture above right);** **apple pie** la tarte aux pommes *tart-o-pomm;* **apple turnover** le chausson aux pommes *shosson o pomm*
appointment le rendez-vous *rondai-voo*
apricot l'abricot [m] *abreeko*
April avril *avreel*
Arab arabe *a-rab*
arcade (amusement) la salle de jeux *sal duh juh*
archaeology l'archéologie [f] *arkai-olojee*
architecture l'architecture [f] *arshee-tektewr*
area (region) la région *raij-yon,* **or (part of town)** le quartier *kart-yai*
argument la dispute *deespewt;* **to have an argument** se disputer *suh deespewtai*
arm le bras *bra*
around autour de *otoor duh*
to arrive arriver *areevai*
art l'art [m] *ar,* **or (school subject)** le dessin *dessan;* **art school** l'école des beaux-arts [f] *aikol dai bo-zar*
artist l'artiste [m/f] *arteest*
as (like) comme *komm;*
as... as aussi... que *o-see... kuh;*
as usual comme d'habitude *komm dabeetewd*
Asia l'Asie [f] *azee*
to ask demander *duh-mondai;*
to ask out inviter *anveetai*
aspirin l'aspirine [f] *aspeereenn;* **an aspirin** un comprimé d'aspirine *un kompreemai daspeereenn*
assistant (in shop, store) le vendeur *vonduhr* f: la vendeuse *vonduhz*
asthma l'asthme [m] *ass-m*
at (time, place) à *a* **or (at X's place)** chez *shai,* **e.g. at Mark's** chez Mark
to attack attaquer *atakai*
attractive séduisant(e) *saidweezon f: saidweezont*
audience le public *pewbleek*
August août *oot*
Australia l'Australie [f] *osstralee*
Australian australien(ne) *osstral-yan f: osstral-yenn*
author l'auteur [m/f] *otuhr*
autumn l'automne [m] *otonn*

apple la pomme

avalanche l'avalanche [f] *avalonsh*
average moyen(ne) *mwa-yan f: mwa-yenn*
avocado l'avocat [m] *avoka*
to avoid éviter *aiveetai*
away à *a,* **e.g. it's 3km away** c'est à 3km
awful affreux *afruh* f: affreuse *afruhz*

back (not front) l'arrière [m] *ar-yair,* **or (part of body)** le dos *do*
backpack le sac à dos *sak a do*
backpacker le routard *rootar*
bad mauvais(e) *movai f: movaiz;* **not bad** pas mal *pa mal;* **really bad** nul(le)* *newl;*
too bad! tant pis! *ton pee*
badge le badge *badj,* **or (small)** le pin's *peennz*
badly mal *mal*
badminton le badminton *bad-meenntonn*
bag le sac *sak*
baker's la boulangerie *boolonj-ree*
ball la balle *bal,* **or (large)** le ballon *ba-lon*
ballet le ballet *balai*
banana la banane *ba-nann*

band (musical) le groupe *groop* (see picture below)
bank (money) la banque *bonk*
bar le bar *bar,* **or (counter)** le comptoir *kontwar*
bargain la bonne affaire *bonn afair*
baseball le base-ball *baiz-bol*
basketball le basket *basskett*
bat (sport) la batte *batt*
bath le bain *ban*
bathroom la salle de bain *sal duh ban*
battery la pile *peel,* **or (car)** la batterie *ba-tree*
to be être *etr* (See Verbs p.45), **or (as in "to be hot/hungry/X years old")** avoir *avwar,* **or (for weather, as in "to be hot/ cold")** faire *fair*
beach la plage *plaj*
beans les haricots [m] *areeko;* **green beans** les haricots verts *areeko vair*
beard la barbe *barb*
beat (rhythm) le rythme *reetm*
beautiful beau† *bo* f: belle *bel*
because parce que *parss-kuh;* **because of** à cause de *a koze duh*
to become devenir *duh-vuh-neer*
bed le lit *lee;* **double bed** le grand lit *gron lee;* **bed and breakfast (guest house)** la chambre d'hôtes *shombr dot*
bedroom la chambre (à coucher) *shombr (a kooshai)*
beetle le scarabée *skarabai*
beef le boeuf *burf*
beer la bière *bee-yair,* **or (on tap)** la (bière) pression *(bee-yair) press-yon,* **or** le demi *duh-mee*
before avant *avon*
beggar le/la mendiant(e) *mond-yon f: mond-yont*
beginner le/la débutant(e) *daibewton f: daibewtont*
beginning le début *daibew*
behind derrière *dair-yair*
Belgium la Belgique *beljeek*
belt la ceinture *santewr*
bend (in the road) le virage *veeraj*

band le groupe

best (person or thing, as in "the best film") le/la meilleur(e) *mai-yuhr,* **or (action, as in "Sam plays best")** le/la mieux *m-yuh;* **the best (as in "it's the best!")** le top* *top*
better (person or thing, as in "this café is better") meilleur(e) *mai-yuhr,* **or (action, as in "Sam plays better")** mieux *m-yuh;* **to feel better** se sentir mieux *suh sonteer m-yuh;* **it is better to...** il vaut mieux... *eel vo m-yuh...*
between entre *ontr*
big grand(e) *gron f: grond*
bike le vélo *vailo;* **racing bike** le vélo de course *vailo duh koorss;* **mountain bike** le vélo tout terrain *vailo too tai-ran,* **or** le VTT *vai tai tai;* **by bike** en vélo *on vailo* (see also picture above right)
biker le motard *mo-tar*
bill (restaurant) l'addition [f] *adeess-yon*
bin (rubbish) la poubelle *poobell*
binoculars les jumelles [f] *jew-mell*
biodegradable biodégradable *bee-o-daigra-dabl*
bird l'oiseau [m] *wazo*
birthday l'anniversaire [m] *anneevair-sair;* **happy birthday** joyeux anniversaire *jwa-yuh-z-anneevair-sair*
biscuit le biscuit *beeskwee*
bit (as in "a bit of cake") le morceau *morso,* **or (as in "a bit tired/hungry")** un peu *un puh*
to bite mordre *mordr,* **or (insect)** piquer *peekai*
bitter amer f: amère *amair*
black noir(e) *nwar*

†beau changes to bel *bell* in front of a [m] word beginning with a vowel, or sometimes an "h", e.g. un bel homme.

blanket la couverture *koovairtewr*
to bleed saigner *sainn-yai*
blind aveugle *avurgl*
blister l'ampoule [f] *ompool*
bloke le type* *teep,* **or** le mec* *mek*
blond blond(e) *blon f: blond;* **the blond guy/girl** le/la blond(e)
blood le sang *son;* **blood pressure** la tension *tonss-yon*
blue bleu(e) *bluh*
blush rougir *roo-jeer*
to boast se vanter *suh vontai,* **or** frimer* *free-mai*
boat (big) le bateau *bato,* **or (small)** la barque *bark;* **to go by boat** prendre le bateau *prondr luh bato*
(see also 'sailing')
body le corps *kor*
boiled bouilli(e) *boo-yee*
bone l'os [m] *oss pl: o,* **or (fish bone)** l'arête [f] *a-rett*
book le livre *leevr*
to book réserver *raizairvai;* **booked up** complet *komplai* f: complète *komplett*
bookshop la librairie *leebrairee*
boot la botte *bott,* **or (for climbing, skiing, walking)** la chaussure *sho-sewr*
border (frontier) la frontière *frontee-air*
bored: **to be bored** s'ennuyer *sonnwee-yai*
boring ennuyeux *onnwee-yuh* f: ennuyeuse *onnwee-yuhz,* **or** rasoir* *razwar*
to borrow emprunter *ompruntai*
boss le/la patron(ne) *patron f: patronn,* **or** le boss*
both tous les deux *too lai duh* f: toutes les deux *toot lai duh*
bottle la bouteille *bootaiy;*

bike le vélo

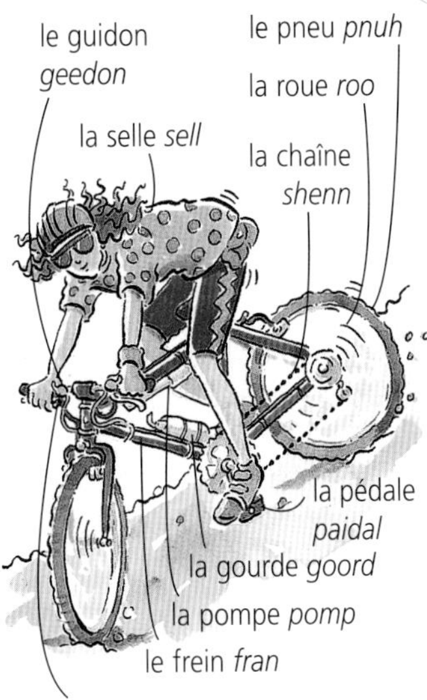

bottle opener le décapsuleur *daikap-sewluhr,* **or** l'ouvre-bouteille [m] *oovr-bootaiy*
bottom (not top) le bas *ba,* **or (of river, pool, glass)** le fond *fon,* **or (part of body)** le derrière *dair-yair*
bowl le bol *bol*
bowling (ten pin) le bowling
boxer shorts des boxers *box-airs*
box office le guichet *geeshai*
boy le garçon *garson*
boyfriend le petit ami *puhtee-tammee*
bra le soutien-gorge *sootee-an gorj,* **or** le soutif** *sooteef*
brakes les freins [m] *fran*
brave courageux *koorajuh* f: courageuse *koorajuhz*
bread le pain *pan;* **wholemeal bread** le pain complet *pan komplai*
to break casser *kassai;*
to break down tomber en panne *tombai on pann;*
to break up (with a person) se séparer *suh saiparai,* **or** rompre* *rompr*
breakfast le petit déjeuner *puhtee daijuhnai,* **or** le petit déj* *ptee daij*
breath l'haleine [f] *a-lenn;* **out of breath** essouflé(e) *aissooflai*
to breathe respirer *respeerai*
bridge le pont *pon*
bright (clever) doué(e) *doo-ai,* **or (colour)** vif *veef* f: vive *veev*
brilliant (fantastic) génial(e) *jainn-yal*
to bring (person) amener *amm-nai,* **or (thing)** apporter *a-portai*
Britain la Grande-Bretagne *grond-bruhtann-yuh*
broke (no money) à sec* *a sek,* **or** fauché(e)* *fo-shai*
brother le frère *frair;* **or** le frangin* *fronjan*
brown brun(e) *brun f: brewnn,* **or** marron *maron,* **or (tanned)** bronzé(e) *bronzai*
bruise le bleu *bluh*
brush la brosse *bross,* **or (paintbrush)** le pinceau *panso*
bug (germ) le microbe *meekrob,* **or (insect)** la bestiole *best-yol*
building le bâtiment *batee-mon*
bull le taureau *toro*
bump (lump on head/ski run) la bosse *boss*
to bump into (something) se cogner contre *suh konn-yai kontr,* **or (someone by chance)** tomber sur *tombai sewr*
to bunk off sécher* *saishai*
to burn brûler *brewlai*
to burst (explode) éclater *aiklatai,* **or (tyre, balloon)** crever *krevai*

bus le bus *bewss;* **bus station** la gare routière *gar root-yair;* **bus stop** l'arrêt de bus [m] *arai duh bewss;* **to take the bus** prendre le bus *prondr luh bewss*
busy (person) occupé(e) *okewpai*
but mais *mai*
butcher's la boucherie *boosh-ree*
butter le beurre *buhr*
to buy acheter *ash-tai*
by (near) près de *prai duh,* **or (as in "saved by someone")** par *par;* **by my/your/him/herself** tout(e) seul(e) *too surl f: toot surl*
bye salut* *sa-lew;* **or** tchao* *tsha-o*

café le café *kafai;* **or** le bar *bar*
cake le gâteau *gato;* **cake shop** la pâtisserie *pateess-ree;* **it's a piece of cake** c'est du gâteau* *sai dew gato*
calculator la calculette *kalkew-lett*
to call appeler *apuhlai;* **to be called** s'appeler *sapuhlai*
calm calme *kalm*
calorie la calorie *kaloree;* **low-calorie** à basses calories *a bass kaloree*
camcorder (video camera) le caméscope *kammaiskop*
camera l'appareil-photo [m] *aparaiy foto* **(see also picture above, on the right)**
to camp camper *kompai;* **to go camping** (aller) faire du camping *(allai) fair dew kompeeng*
campsite le camping *kompeeng* **(see also picture on the right)**
can (of fruit/drink) la boîte *bwat;* **can opener** l'ouvre-boîte [m] *oovr-bwat*
can (to be able to) pouvoir *poovwar* **(see Verbs p.45), or (to know how to)** savoir *savwar*
Canada le Canada *kannada*
canal le canal *kannal*
to cancel annuler *annewlai*
candle la bougie *boojee*
canoe le canoë *kanno-ai,* **or (kayak)** le kayak; **to go canoeing** faire du canoë/kayak
cap (hat) la casquette *kasskett*
capital (city) la capitale *kapeetal*
captain le capitaine *kapeetenn*
car la voiture *vwa-tewr,* **or** la bagnole* *bann-yol;* **car park** le parking *parkeeng*
card la carte *kart;* **credit card** la carte de crédit *kart duh kraidee;* **a game of cards** une partie de cartes *ewnn partee duh kart*
care: I don't care! ça m'est égal! *sa mai-taigal,* **or** je m'en fous!** *juh mon foo*
career la carrière *kar-yair*
careful prudent(e) *prewdon f: prewdont;* **to be careful** faire attention *fair atonss-yon*
carnival le carnaval *kar-naval*
carrot la carotte *ka-rott*
to carry porter *portai*
cartoon le dessin animé *dessan annee-mai*
case in case au cas où *o ka oo*
cash (money) l'argent liquide [m] *arjon leekeed,* **or** le liquide; **cash dispenser/cashpoint machine** le distributeur de billets *dee- stree-bewtuhr duh bee-yai*

castle le château *sha-to*
casual (relaxed, informal) décontracté(e) *daikontraktai*
cat le chat *sha*
to catch attraper *atrapai*
cathedral la cathédrale *kataidral*
Catholic catholique *katoleek*
cave (small) la caverne *kavairnn,* **or (large)** la grotte *grott*
caving la spéléologie *spailai-olojee,* **or** la spéléo
CD le CD *saidai;* **CD player** le lecteur de CD *lektuhr duh sai dai*
to celebrate fêter *fettai*
cellar la cave *kav*
cemetery le cimetière *seemt-yair*
centre le centre *sontr*
century le siècle *see-aikl*
cereal les céréales [f] *sai-rai-al*
chair la chaise *shaiz,* **or (with arms)** le fauteuil *fotuh-y*
champion le/la champion(ne) *shomp-yon f: shomp-yonn*
championship le championnat *shomp-yonna*

chance (accident) le hasard *azar,* **or (opportunity)** l'occasion [f] *okaz-yon,* **or (risk)** le risque *reesk;* **by chance** par hasard *par azar*
change le changement *shonj-mon,* **or (money)** la monnaie *monnai*
to change changer *shonjai*
changing-room le vestiaire *vest-yair*
channel (TV) la chaîne *shenn;* **the Channel** la Manche *monsh;* **the Channel tunnel** le tunnel sous la Manche *tew-nel soo la monsh;* **the Channel Islands** les îles anglo-normandes [f] *eel onglo-normond*
chaos la pagaille* *pag-eye*
character (personality) le caractère *karaktair,* **or (person in cartoon etc.)** le personnage *pairsonnaj*
charity (organization) l'organisme de charité [m] *organneezm duh shareetai*
charter (plane, flight) le charter *shartair*
to chat bavarder *bavardai;* **to chat up** draguer** *dragai,* **or** brancher** *bronshai*
cheap pas cher f: pas chère *pa shair,* **or** bon marché *bon marshai*
cheaper moins cher f: moins chère *mwan chair*
to cheat (at cards etc.) tricher *treeshai*
to check (a fact, date) vérifier *vaireef-yai,* **or (a passport, ticket)** contrôler *kontrolai;* **to check in (luggage)** enregistrer *onruh-jeess-trai*
check-in (at airport) l'enregistrement [m] *onruh-jeess-truhmon*
check-out (cash register) la caisse *kess*
cheeky gonflé(e)* *gonflai*
cheers (à ta/votre) santé *(a ta/votr) sontai,* **or** à la tienne/vôtre* *a la tee-enn/ votr*
cheer up! courage! *kooraj*
cheese le fromage *fromaj*
chemist's la pharmacie *farmassee*
cheque le chèque *shek;* **cheque-book** le chéquier *shaik-yai*
cherry la cerise *suhreez*
chess les échecs [m] *aishek*
chest (part of body) la poitrine *pwatreenn*
chewing gum le chewing-gum *shweeng-gomm*
chicken le poulet *poolai*
child l'enfant [m/f] *onfon*
chips les frites [f] *freet*
chocolate le chocolat *shokola;* **hot chocolate** le chocolat chaud *shokola sho*
choice le choix *shwa*
choir le choeur *kuhr*
to choose choisir *shwazeer*
chop (e.g. pork/lamb) la côtelette *kotlett*
Christian chrétien(ne) *krait-yan f: krait-yenn*
Christmas Noël *no-ell*
to chuck (throw) balancer* *balonssai,* **or (finish with a boy/girlfriend)** laisser tomber *laissai tombai,* **or** plaquer** *plakai*
church l'église [f] *aigleez*
cider le cidre *seedr*
cigarette la cigarette *seegarett,* **or** la clope** *klop*
cinema le cinéma *see-naima,* **or** le ciné*, **or** le cinoche* *see-nosh*
circus le cirque *seerk*
city la ville *veel*
classical classique *klasseek*
clean propre *propr*
clever intelligent(e) *anteleejon f: anteleejont,* **or (cunning)** malin *malan* f: maligne *maleenn,* **or (gifted)** doué(e) *doo-ai*

campsite le camping

climbing l'escalade [f] **or** la grimpe*

le rocher *roshai*

le mousqueton *moosk-ton*

le grimpeur *grampuhr*

le casque *kask*

la sangle *sangl*

la magnésie *mann-yaizee*

le sac à magnésie *sak a mann-yaizee*

le baudrier *bodree-ai*

le chausson d'escalade *shosson deskalad*

la corde *kord*

cliff la falaise *falaiz*
to climb grimper *grampai*
climber le grimpeur *grampuhr* f: la grimpeuse *grampurz*
climbing l'escalade [f] *eskalad,* **or** la grimpe* *gramp,* **or (mountain-climbing)** l'alpinisme [m] *alpee-neezm,* **or (rock-climbing on boulders)** la varappe *varap* **(see also picture on the left)**
cloakroom le vestiaire *vest-yair*
close près de *prai duh,* **or (feeling)** proche *prosh;* **close by** tout près *too prai*
to close fermer *fairmai*
closed fermé(e) *fairmai*
clothes les vêtements [m] *vetmon,* **or** les fringues* [f] *frang*
cloud le nuage *new-aj*
club le club *klerb,* **or (night-club)** la boîte* (de nuit) *bwat (duh nwee)*
clubbing: to go clubbing aller en boîte* *allai on bwat*
coach (bus) le car *kar,* **or (trainer)** l'entraîneur [m/f] *ontrai-nuhr*
coast la côte *kote*
coat le manteau *monto*
coconut la noix de coco *nwa duh koko*
code (post/entry code) le code *kod,* **or (for phoning)** l'indicatif [m] *andeekateef*
co-ed (school) mixte *meekst*
coffee le café *kafai;* **a black coffee** un café (noir) *un kafai (nwar);* **a coffee with milk/ cream** un (café-)crème *kremm;* **a decaffeinated coffee** un déca *daika*
coin la pièce *pee-ess*
coincidence la coïncidence *ko-ansseedonss*
cold froid(e) *frwa* f: *frwad,* **or (chilled)** frais *frai* f: fraîche *fraish;* **to be cold (person)** avoir froid *avwar frwa,* **or (weather) it is cold** il fait froid *eel fai frwa;* **to have cold feet (about something)** avoir la trouille** *avwar la troo-yuh*
cold (illness) le rhume *rewmm;* **to have a cold** être enrhumé(e) *etr onrew-mai*
to collect (stamps etc.) collectionner *koleks-yonnai*
colour la couleur *kooluhr*
comb le peigne *penn-yuh*
to come venir *vuh-neer;* **to come back** revenir *ruh-vuh-neer;* **to come in** entrer *ontrai*
comfortable confortable *konfortabl;* **to be/feel comfortable** être à l'aise *etr a laiz*
comic book la bande dessinée *bond desseennai,* **or** la BD *bai dai*
common courant(e) *kooron* f: *kooront;* **common sense** le bon sens *bon sonss*
compass (small) la boussole *boossol* **or (large)** le compas *kompa*
competition le concours *konkoor,* **or (people you are up against)** la concurrence *konkew-ronss*
to complain se plaindre *suh plandr*
completely complètement *komplaitmon*
compulsory obligatoire *oblee-ga-twar*
computer l'ordinateur [m] *ordee-natuhr;* **computer studies** l'informatique [f] *anfor-mateek*
concert le concert *konssair*
to confess avouer *av-wai*
to confuse confondre *konfondr*

congratulations félicitations *faileesseetass-yon*
connection (plane, train) la correspondance *korespondonss*
conservation la défense de l'environnement *daifonss duh lonveeronn-mon*
constipated constipé(e) *konsteepai*
consulate le consulat *konssewla*
to contact contacter *kontaktai*
contact lens la lentille (de contact) *lonteey (duh kontakt)*; **soft/hard lens** la lentille souple/dure *lonteey soopl/dewr*; **cleansing/rinsing solution** la solution de décontamination/neutralisation *solewss-yon duh dai-konta-mee-nass-yon/nuh-tralee-zass-yon*
contagious contagieux *kontaj-yuh* f: contagieuse *kontaj-yurz*
contemporary contemporain(e) *kontomporan* *f: kontemporenn*
to continue continuer *kontee-newai*
conversation la conversation *konvairsass-yon*
to cook faire de la cuisine *fair duh la kweezeenn*
cookery la cuisine *la kweezeenn*
cool (trendy, relaxed) cool*
to cope se débrouiller *suh daibroo-yai*, **or (to face up to)** faire face à *fair fass a*
to copy copier *kop-yai*
cork le bouchon *booshon*
corkscrew le tire-bouchon *teer-booshon*
corner le coin *kwan*
correct correct(e) *korekt*
Corsica la Corse *korss*
cosmopolitan cosmopolite *kozmopoleet*
to cost coûter *kootai*
cotton (material) le coton *koton*; **cotton wool** le coton
country (nation) le pays *pai-ee*, **or (countryside)** la campagne *kompann-yuh*
course (series of lessons) le cours *koor*, **or (meal)** le plat *pla*; **first course** l'entrée [f] *ontrai*; **of course** bien sûr *bee-an sewr*
court (tennis, squash) le court *koor*, **or (basketball, volleyball)** le terrain *tairan*
cousin le/la cousin(e) *koozan* *f: koozeenn*
to cover couvrir *koovreer*
cow la vache *vash*
coward le lâche *lash*
to crack (lose control, give in) craquer *krakai*; **to crack a joke** sortir une blague *sorteer ewnn blag*; **to crack up (laugh)** être écroulé(e)* (de rire) *etr aikroolai (duh reer)*
cramp la crampe *kromp*
crazy fou *foo* f: folle *fol*, **or** cinglé(e)* *sanglai*, **or** dingue* *dang*; **to drive crazy** rendre fou/dingue* *rondr foo/dang*; **to be crazy about (a person)** être fou de *etr foo duh*, **or (a thing)** adorer *adorai*; **you must be crazy!** ça va pas la tête?* *sa va pa la tet*
credit card (see 'card')
creepy qui donne la chair de poule *kee donn la shair duh pooll*
cress le cresson *krai-son*
cricket (sport) le cricket *cricket*, **or (insect)** le grillon *gree-yon*
crime le crime *kreemm*
crisis la crise *kreez*
crisps les chips [f] *sheeps*
to criticize critiquer *kreeteekai*
cross (angry) fâché(e) *fashai*, **or (sign)** la croix *krwa*
to cross traverser *travairsai*
crossing (by ferry etc.) la traversée *travairsai* **(see also 'pedestrian')**
crossroads le carrefour *karfoor*
crossword les mots croisés [m] *mo krwazai*
crow (bird) le corbeau kor-bo
cruel cruel(le) *krew-ell*
crush: I've got a crush on him/her il/elle me fait craquer* *eel/ell muh fai krakai*
to cry (weep) pleurer *pluhrai*
cucumber le concombre *konkombr*
cult le culte *kewlt*
cultural culturel(le) *kewltewrell*
culture la culture *kewltewr*
cup la tasse *tass*
cupboard le placard *plakar*
curious curieux *kewr-yuh* f: curieuse *kewr-yuhz*
custom la coutume *kootewmm*
customer le/la client(e) *klee-on* *f: klee-ont*
customs la douane *dwann*
to cut couper *koopai*

to dance dancer *donsai*
dancer le danseur *dansuhr* f: la danseuse *dansuhz*
dangerous dangereux *donj-ruh* f: dangereuse *donj-ruhz*
to dare (risk) oser *ozai*, **or (challenge)** défier *daifee-ai*
dark sombre *sombr*, **or (colour)** foncé(e) *fonsai* **(see also 'hair' picture); it is dark** il fait noir *eel fai nwar*
dart la fléchette *flaishett*
date la date *dat*, **or (meeting with boy/girlfriend)** le rendez-vous *rondai-voo*, **or** le rancard** *ronkar*; **date of birth** la date de naissance *dat duh naissonss*; **up to date (current)** à jour *a joor*; **out of date (no longer valid)** périmé(e) *paireemai*

day le jour *joor;* **the next day** le lendemain *lond-man;* **the day before** la veille *vaiy;* **day off** le jour de congé *joor duh konjai*
dead mort(e) *mor f: mort*
deaf sourd(e) *soor f: soord*
dear cher f: chère *shair*
decaffeinated décaféiné(e) *dai-kafai-eennai*
December décembre *daissombr*
to decide décider *daisseedai*
deck (on boat) le pont *pon;* **deck chair** la chaise longue *shaiz long,* **or** le transat *tronzat*
deep profond(e) *profon f: profond*
degree (as in "90°") le degré *duhgrai,* **or (university)** la licence *leessonss*
delay le retard *ruhtar*
delicatessen (for ready-made dishes) le traiteur *traituhr,* **or (for salami, pâté, etc.)** la charcuterie *sharkewtree*
delicious délicieux *daileess-yuh* f: délicieuse *daileess-yuhz*
democracy la démocratie *dai-mokrassee*
demonstration la manifestation *manneefestass-yon,* **or (demo)** la manif*
denim (made of denim) en jean *on djeenn*
dentist le/la dentiste *donteest*
deodorant le déodorant *dai-odoron*
department store le grand magasin *gron magazan*
departure le départ *daipar;* **departure lounge** la salle d'embarquement *sal dombark-mon*
to depend dépendre *daipondr*
deposit (money left as guarantee) la caution *koss-yon,* **or (money given in advance)** les arrhes [f] *ar*
depressing déprimant(e) *daipreemon f: daipreemont*
to describe décrire *daikreer*

diving la plongée

les palmes [f] *palmm*
la combinaison *kombee-naizon*
la bouteille d'oxygène *bootaiy dokseejenn*
le tuba *tewba*
la plongeuse plonjuhz
le masque *mask*
le détendeur *daitonduhr*
la console *konsol*
la ceinture de plomb *santewr duh plom*
le gilet stabilisateur *jeelai stabeeleezatuhr*

desk le bureau *bewro*
dessert le dessert *daissair*
detail le détail *dai-tie*
detour le détour *daitoor*
diabetic diabétique *dee-abaiteek*
dialect le dialecte *dee-alekt*
dialling tone la tonalité *tonnaleetai* **(see also 'code')**
diarrhoea la diarrhée *dee-arai*
diary l'agenda [m] *ajenda,* **or (private book)** le journal *joor-nal*
dice le dé *dai*
dictionary le dictionnaire *deeksee-onnair,* **or** le dico* *deeko*
diesel (fuel) le gazole *ga-zol*
diet le régime *raijeemm;* **to go on a diet** se mettre au régime *suh metr o raijeemm*
different différent(e) *deefairon f: deefairont*
difficult difficile *deefeesseel*
to dine dîner *dee-nai*
dining room la salle à manger *sal a monjai*
dinner (evening) le dîner *dee-nai,* **or (midday)** le déjeuner *daijuh-nai*
direction la direction *deereks-yon*
director (of film) le metteur en scène *metuhr on senn*
dirty sale *sal,* **or (rude)** grossier *gross-yai* f: grossière *gross-yair;* **to get dirty** se salir *suh saleer*
disabled handicapé(e) *ondeekapai*
disadvantage (drawback) l'inconvénient [m] *ankonvenn-yon*
to disappear disparaître *dees-par-etr*
disappointed déçu(e) *daissew*

disaster la catastrophe *katastrof*
disc jockey le disc-jockey *deesk jokai*
disco la discothèque *deeskotek*
discount la réduction *raidewks-yon*
discrimination la discrimination *deeskree-mee-nass-yon*
to discuss discuter *deeskewtai*
discussion la discussion *dees-koos-yon*
disgusting dégoûtant(e) *daigooton f: daigootont,* **or** dégueulasse** *dai-guh-lass*
dish le plat *pla*
distance la distance *deestonss;* **in the/from a distance** au/de loin *o/duh lwan*
to dive plonger *plonjai*
diving la plongée *plonjai;* **scuba diving** la plongée sous-marine *plonjai soo-mareenn* **(see also picture on the left); diving board** le plongeoir *plonjwar*
divorced divorcé(e) *deevorsai*
dizzy: to be/feel dizzy avoir la tête qui tourne *avwar la tet kee toornn*
to do faire *fair* **(see Verbs p.45), to do up (fasten)** attacher *atashai*
doctor le médecin *med-san,* **or** le docteur *doktuhr*
dodgy (dubious) louche *loosh,* **or (risky)** risqué(e) *reeskai*
dog le chien *shee-an*
dole: on the dole au chômage *o shomaj*
door la porte *port*
double double *doobl,* **or (for two people)** pour deux personnes *poor duh pairsonn*
down: to go/walk down descendre *daissondr;* **to be/ feel down** être déprimé(e) *etr depreemai,* **or** avoir le cafard* *avwar luh kafar*
draw (same score) le match nul *match newl*
to draw (a picture) dessiner *daissee-nai*
dream le rêve *rev*
dress la robe *rob*
to dress (get dressed) s'habiller *sabee-yai*
drink la boisson *bwasson;* **let's go for a drink** on va prendre un verre/un pot* *on va prondr un vair/un po*
to drink boire *bwar*
to drive conduire *kondweer,* **or (to go by car)** aller en voiture *allai on vwatewr;* **to drive along/around** rouler *roolai*
driver le chauffeur *sho-fuhr*
to drop (let fall) laisser tomber *laissai tombai,* **or (let go of)** lâcher *lashai;* **to drop in** passer *passai;* **to drop off (as in "drop me off at the corner")** déposer *daipozai;* **to drop out (of college/a competition)** abandonner *abondonnai*
drug la drogue *drog;* **drug addict** le/la drogué(e) *drogai;* **to take drugs** se droguer *suh drogai*
dry sec *sek* f: sèche *sesh*
to dry sécher *saishai*
dubbed doublé(e) *dooblai*
dump (for rubbish) la décharge *daisharj,* **or (dull, awful place)** le trou* *troo;* **to be down in the dumps** broyer du noir *brwa-yai dew nwar*
dungarees la salopette *salopett*
during pendant *pondon*
DVD DVD *day-vey-day*
DVD player le lecteur de DVD *lektuhr duh day-vey-day*
dying: to be dying to (do something) mourir d'envie de *mooreer donvee duh;* **to be dying of hunger/thirst** mourir de faim/soif *mooreer duh fam/swaf*

each chaque *shak,* **or (each one)** chacun(e) *shakun f: shakewnn*
eagle l'aigle [m/f] *ai-gl*
ear l'oreille [f] *oraiy* **(see also 'to ache' picture)**
early tôt *toe,* **or (ahead of time)** en avance *onnavonss*
to earn (money) gagner *gan-yai*
earphones les écouteurs [m] *aikootuhr*
Earth (the) la Terre *tair*
east l'est [m] *est*
Easter Pâques *pak*
easy facile *fasseel*
easy-going décontracté(e) *daikontraktai*
to eat manger *monjai,* **or** bouffer** *boofai Eat up! Mangez! monjai*
ecology l'écologie [f] *aikolojee*
education l'éducation [f] *aidewkass-yon;* **higher education** les études supérieures [f] *aitewd sewpair-yuhr*
egg l'oeuf [m] *urf pl: uh* (see also picture on p.14)
elbow le coude *kood*
election l'élection [f] *aileks-yon*
electric électrique *ailek-treek*
electricity l'électricité [f] *ailek-treesseetai*
elevator l'ascenseur [m] *assonsuhr*

e-mail le courrier électronique *kuhr-yai ailek-troneek* **or** un e-mail *ee-mail*
embarrassing gênant(e) *jennon f: jennont;* **how embarrassing!** quelle honte! *kell ont*
embassy l'ambassade [f] *ombassad*
emergency l'urgence [f] *ewrjonss;* **emergency exit** la sortie de secours *sortee duh suhkoor*
empty vide *veed*
end (of story) la fin *fan,* **or (of road, finger)** le bout *boo*
engine le moteur *motuhr*
England l'Angleterre [f] *ongluhtair*
English anglais(e) *onglai f: onglaiz;* **in English** en anglais
to enjoy yourself s'amuser *samoozai*
enough assez *assai;* **I've had enough** j'en ai assez *jonnai assai*
entertainment guide le guide des spectacles *geed dai spektakl*
envelope l'enveloppe [f] *onvlop*
environment l'environnement [m] *onveeronn-mon*
envy l'envie (f) *on-vee*
epileptic épileptique *aipeelepteek;* **epileptic fit** la crise d'épilepsie *kreez daipeelepsee*
equal égal(e) *aigal*
escalator l'escalator [m] *eskalator*
essential indispensable *andeesponssabl*
EU (European Union) l'Union Européenne *loon-yon uhropai-enn*
Europe l'Europe [f] *uhrop;* **eastern Europe** l'Europe de l'est [m] *duh lest* **western Europe** l'Europe occidentale *okseedontall*
European européen(ne) *uhropai-an f: uhropai-enn*
evening le soir *swar*
everybody tout le monde *too luh mond*
everything tout *too;* **everything else** tout le reste *too luh rest*
everywhere partout *partoo*
to exaggerate exagérer *aigzajairai*
exam l'examen [m] *aigzaman,* **or** l'exam*
example l'exemple [m] *aigzompl;* **for example** par exemple
excellent excellent(e) *aiksailon f: aiksailont*
except sauf *sof*
excess: excess baggage l'excédent de bagages [m] *aiksaidon duh bagaj;* **excess fare** le supplément *sewp-laimon*
exchange (money) le change *shonj,* **or (holiday)** l'échange [m] *aishonj;* **foreign exchange office** le bureau de change *bewro duh shonj;* **exchange rate** le taux de change *toe duh shonj*
excited excité(e) *aikseetai;* **to get excited** s'exciter *saikseetai*
exciting passionnant(e) *passyonnon f: passyonnont*
excuse l'excuse [f] *aiks-kewz;* **excuse me** excusez-moi *aiks-kewzai-mwa*
exercise l'exercice [m] *aigzairseess*
exhausted épuisé(e) *aipweezai,* **or** crevé(e)** *kruhvai*
exhibition l'exposition [f] *aikspozeess-yon*
exit la sortie *sortee*
exotic exotique *aigzoteek*
expensive cher f: chère *shair*
experience l'expérience [f] *aikspair-yonss*
to explain expliquer *aiks-pleekai*
to explore explorer *aiks-plorai*
extra supplémentaire *sewp-laimontair*
eye l'oeil [m] *uh-yuh* pl: les yeux *yuh*

fabulous super *sewpair*

egg l'oeuf

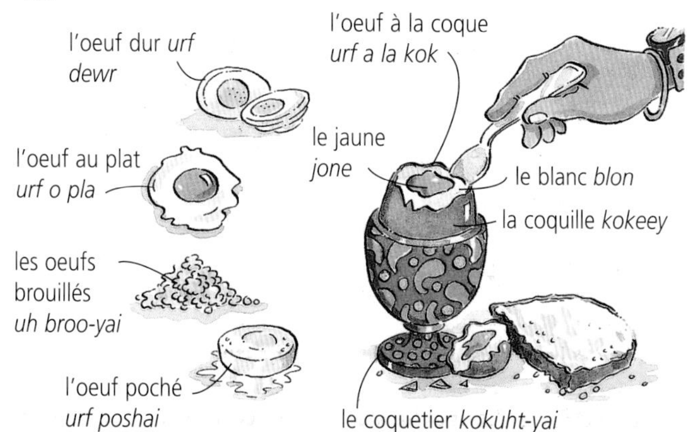

face le visage *veezaj*
to fail (exam) rater *rat-ai*
to faint s'évanouir *saivannoo-eer,* **or** tomber dans les pommes* *tombai don lai pomm*
fair (just) juste *jewst*
faithful fidèle *fee-dell*
to fall tomber *tombai;*
to fall for (a person) tomber amoureux de *tombai amoo-ruh duh* f: ...amoureuse... *amooruhz...,* **or (a trick)** se faire avoir* *suh fair avwar;*
to fall out with (a person) se fâcher avec *suh fashai avek*
family la famille *fameey*
famous (a star) célèbre *sailebr,* **or (well-known)** (bien) connu(e) *(bee-an) konnew*
fan (admirer) le/la fan *fann,* **or (enthusiast)** le/la mordu(e) *mordew,* **or** le/la passionné(e) *pass-yonnai*
to fancy (in French you say that "someone appeals to you") plaire à *plair a,* **e.g. Luke fancies her** elle plaît à Luc; **do you fancy (doing something)?** ça te dit de...? *sa tuh dee duh...*
fantastic génial(e) *jainn-yall*
far loin *lwan*
fare le tarif *tareef;* **full fare** le plein tarif *plan tareef;* **reduced fare** le tarif réduit *tareef raidwee*
fashion la mode *mod*
fashionable à la mode *a la mod*
fast (quick) rapide *rapeed,* **or (quickly)** vite *veet*
fat (on meat) le gras *gra,* **or (large)** gros(se) *gro f: gross;*
to get fat grossir *grosseer*
father le père *pair*
favourite préféré(e) *praifairai*
February février *faivree-ai*
fed: to be fed up en avoir marre* *on-navwar mar*
to feel (as in "to feel happy/good" etc.) se sentir *suh sonteer,* **or (as in "to feel hot/hungry" etc.)** avoir *avwar;* **to feel like (doing something)** avoir envie de *avwar onvee duh*
feminist le/la féministe *fai-mee-neest*
ferry le ferry *fairee*
fever la fièvre *fee-aivr*
few peu de *puh duh;* **a few (as in "I'd like a few")** quelques-un(e)s *kelkuh-zun f: ...zewnn,* **or (as in "a few cakes")** quelques *kelkuh*
field le champ *shon*
fig la figue *feeg*
fight la bagarre* *bagar,* **or (organized)** le combat *komba*
to fight se battre *suh batr*
figure: to have a good figure être bien fait(e) *etr bee-an fai f: ...fait*
to fill remplir *rompleer;* **to fill up (with fuel)** faire le plein *fair luh plan*
film (at cinema) le film *feelm,* **or (in camera)** la pellicule *paileekewl*
to find trouver *troovai;*
to find out (get information) se renseigner *suh ronsenn-yai,* **or (discover)** découvrir *daikoovreer*
fine (penalty) l'amende [f] *ammond,* **or (OK)** bien *bee-an* **(see also 'weather')**
finger le doigt *dwa*
to finish finir *feeneer*
fire le feu *fuh;* **fire brigade** les (sapeurs) pompiers [m] *(sapuhr) pomp-yai;* **fire exit** la sortie de secours *sortee duh suhkoor*
fireworks le feu d'artifice *fuh darteefeess*
first (the first) le premier *pruhm-yai* f: la première *pruhm-yair,* **or (at first)** d'abord *dabor*
first aid les premiers secours [m] *pruhm-yai suhkoor;* **first aid kit** la trousse à pharmacie *trooss a farmassee* **(see also picture p.16)**
fish le poisson *pwasson*
fishing la pêche *pesh;* **to go fishing** aller à la pêche *allai a la pesh*
fit (tantrum) la crise *kreez,* **or (physically fit)** en (pleine) forme *on (plenn) form;* **he's really fit (good-looking)** c'est un beau mec* *sait un bo mek;*
to be in fits (of laughter) avoir le fou rire *avwar luh foo reer*
to fit aller *allai* **e.g. does it fit?** ça te va?, **it fits me well** ça me va bien
to fix (mend) réparer *raiparai,* **or (arrange a time/date)** fixer *feeksai*
fizzy (drink) gazeux *gazuh* f: gazeuse *gazuhz*
flat (apartment) l'appartement [m] *apart-mon,* **or** l'appart* *apart,* **or (not round)** plat(e) *pla f: plat,* **or (tyre)** dégonflé(e) *daigonflai*
flavour le goût *goo,* **or (of ice cream)** le parfum *parfam*
flea market le marché aux puces *marshai o pewss*
flight le vol *vol;* **flight attendant** l'hôtesse de l'air (f) *o-tess duh lair,* **or (male)** le steward *stewar*
flirt le dragueur* *draguhr* f: la dragueuse* *draguhz*
to flirt draguer* *dragai,* **or** brancher** *bronshai*
floor (level) l'étage [m] *aitaj*
flop (failure) le fiasco *fee-asko,* **or** le bide* *beed*
flour la farine *fareen*
flower la fleur *fluhr*
flu la grippe *greep*
fluently couramment *kooramon*

fly la mouche *moosh*
to fly voler *volai,* **or (go by plane)** aller en avion *allai onnav-yon*
to follow suivre *sweevr*
food la nourriture *nooree-tewr,* **or** la bouffe** *boof;*
food-poisoning l'intoxication alimentaire [f] *antok-seekass-yon alee-montair*
foot le pied *pee-ai;* **on foot** à pied; **to put your foot in it** faire une gaffe* *fair ewnn gaff*
football le football *foot-bol,* **or** le foot*; **American football** le football américain *foot-bol ammaireekan* **(see also picture on the right)**
for pour *poor*
forbidden interdit(e) *antairdee f: antairdeet*
foreigner l'étranger *aitronjai* f: l'étrangère *aitronjair*
forest la forêt *forai*
to forget oublier *ooblee-ai*
to forgive pardonner *pardonnai*
fork la fourchette *foorshett*
fountain la fontaine *fontenn*
frame (picture, bike) le cadre *kadr,* **or (glasses)** la monture *montewr*
France la France *fronss*
to freak out (lose your cool) craquer* *krakai,* **or** flipper** *fleepai*
free libre *leebr,* **or (no charge)** gratuit(e) *gratwee f: gratweet*
to freeze geler *juhlai;* **it's freezing** ça caille** *sa ka-yuh*
French français(e) *fronssai f: fronssaiz;* **in French** en français; **French fries** les frites [f] *freet*
fresh frais *frai* f: fraîche *fraish*
Friday vendredi [m] *vondruhdee*
fridge le frigo *freego*
friend l'ami(e) [m/f] *amee,* **or** le copain* *kopan* f: la copine* *kopeenn*
friendly sympathique *sampateek,* **or** sympa*
frightened: to be frightened avoir peur *avwar puhr*
from de *duh*
front (of car, train) l'avant [m] *avon,* **or (of dress, building)** le devant *duhvon;* **in front of** devant
fruit le fruit *frwee*
full plein(e) *plan f: plenn,* **or (hotel etc.)** complet *komplai* f: complète *komplett;* **I'm full** j'ai assez mangé *jai assai monjai*
fun amusant(e) *ammewzon f: ammewzont,* **or** marrant(e)* *maron f: maront;* **to have fun** s'amuser *sammewzai,* **or** se marrer** *suh marrai;* **(just) for fun** pour rire *poor reer;* **to make fun of** se moquer de *suh mokai duh*
funfair la fête foraine *fett forenn*
funny (ha! ha!) drôle *drol,* **or (peculiar)** bizarre *beezar*
fuss: to make a fuss faire tout un plat* *fair too-tun pla*

gallery la galerie *galree*
game le jeu *juh,* **or (football, hockey)** le match, **or (tennis, cards)** la partie *partee*
garage le garage *garaj*
garden le jardin *jardan*
garlic l'ail [m] *eye*
gas le gaz *gaz*
gate (in airport) la porte *port*
gear (car, bike) la vitesse *veetess*
general général *jai-nairal;* **in general** en général
generous généreux *jai-nairuh* f: généreuse *jai-nairuhz*
geography la géographie *jai-o-grafee*
German allemand(e) *al-mon f: al-mond*
Germany l'Allemagne [f] *al-mann-yuh*
to get (buy) acheter *ashtai,* **or (fetch)** aller chercher *allai shairshai,* **or (obtain)** avoir *avwar,* **or (take a train/ taxi)** prendre *prondr,* **or (understand)** saisir *saizeer,* **or** piger* *peejai;* **to get away (escape)** s'échapper *saishappai;* **to get off (bus, train)** descendre *daissondr;* **to get on (bus, train)** monter *montai;*

first aid kit la trousse à pharmacie

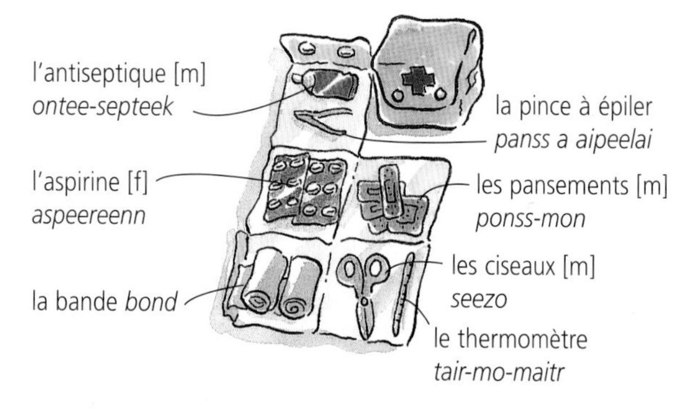

football (soccer) le football

football (American) le football américain

to get along/on with (like) s'entendre avec *sontondr avek;* **to get up** se lever *suh luh-vai*
girl la fille *feey,* **or (derogatory)** la nana* *na-na*
girlfriend la petite amie *puhteet-amee*
to give donner *donnai,* **or (as a gift, treat)** offrir *ofreer,* **or (to pass) passer** *passai;* **to give back** rendre *rondr;* **to give up** abandonner *abondonnai;* **to give way (yield)** céder *saidai*
glass le verre *vair*
glasses (spectacles) les lunettes [f] *lew-nett*
glove le gant *gon*
go (turn) le tour *toor;* **your go** à toi *a twa;* **whose go is it?** c'est à qui le tour? *sai-ta kee luh toor;*
go-kart le kart *karrt*
to go aller *allai* **(see Verbs p.44), or (leave)** partir *parteer;* **go ahead!** vas-y! *va-zee;* **to go away** s'en aller *sonn-allai;* **to go back** retourner *ruhtoor-nai;* **to go in** entrer *ontrai;* **to go out** sortir *sorteer*
goal le but *bewt*
goalkeeper le gardien de but *gardee-an duh bewt*
god le dieu *dee-uh*
good bon(ne) *bon f: bonn,* **or (well-behaved)** sage *saj,* **or (weather)** beau *bo*;
good-looking beau *bo* f: belle *bell;* **good morning/ afternoon** bonjour *bonjoor;* **good evening** bonsoir *bonswar;* **good night** bonne nuit *bonn nwee*
goodbye au revoir *o ruhvwar,* **or** salut* *sa-lew*
gooseberry: **to be a gooseberry** tenir la chandelle *tuh-neer la shondell*
gossip les commérages [m] *kommairaj,* **or (person)** la commère *kommair*
to gossip bavarder *bavardai,* **or (maliciously)** faire des commérages *fair dai kommairaj*
government le gouvernement *goovair-nuh-mon*
graffiti les graffiti [m] *grafeetee,* **or** les tags [m] *tag*
gram le gramme *gram*
grandfather le grand-père *gron pair*
grandmother la grand-mère *gron mair*
grant la bourse *boorss*
grapefruit le pamplemousse *pompl-mooss*
grape le raisin *raizan;* **bunch of grapes** la grappe de raisin *grap duh raizan;* **grape harvest** les vendanges [f] *vondonj*
grass l'herbe [f] *airb*
grateful reconnaissant(e) *ruhkonnaisson f: ruhkonnaissont*
great (terrific) super *sewpair*
green vert(e) *vair f: vairt*
grey gris(e) *gree f: greez*
grilled grillé(e) *gree-yai*
gross (horrible) dégoûtant *dai-goo-tont* **or** dégueulasse** *dai-guh-lass*
grotty (not very nice) minable* *meennabl;* **to feel grotty** être mal fichu* *etr mal feeshoo*
ground la terre *tair;* **on the ground** par terre;
ground floor le rez-de-chaussée *rai-duh-shossai*
group le groupe *groop*
to grow (person, thing) grandir *grondeer,* **or (plant)** pousser *poossai*
to guess deviner *duhvee-nai*

guest l'invité(e) [m/f] *anveetai*
guide (person, or book) le guide *geed*
guilty coupable *koopabl*
guitar la guitare *geetar*
guy le gars* *ga,* **or** le type* *teep*
gym (gymnastics) la gym *jeem,* **or (gymnasium)** le gymnase *jeem-naz*
gypsy le/la gitan(e) *jeetan f: jeetann*

habit l'habitude [f] *abeetewd*
to haggle marchander *marshondai*
hair (on head) les cheveux [m] *shuh-vuh,* **or (on body)** les poils [m] *pwal;* **hairstyle** la coiffure *kwafewr* **(see also picture on the right)**
hairdresser le coiffeur *kwafuhr* f: la coiffeuse *kwafurz*
half la moitié *mwat-yai,* **or (with numbers)** demi(e) *duh-mee;* **half a kilo** un demi-kilo *un duh-mee keelo;* **half an hour** une demi-heure *ewnn duh-mee uhr* **(see also 'time' picture); a half bottle** une demi-bouteille *ewnn duh-mee bootaiy;* **half asleep/dressed** à moitié endormi(e)/habillé(e) *a mwat-yai ondormee/abee-yai;*
half-time la mi-temps *mee-ton*
ham le jambon *jombon*
hamburger le hamburger *amboorguhr*
hand la main *man;* **by hand** à la main; **handmade** fait(e) à la main *fai a la man f: fait...;* **helping hand** le coup de main *koo duh ma*
to hang (something up) accrocher *akroshai;* **to hang around/out** traîner* *trainnai;*
to hang up (phone) raccrocher *rakroshai*
hang-gliding le deltaplane *del-taplann*
hanger (clothes) le cintre *santr*
to happen se passer *suh passai,* **or** arriver *areevai*
happy heureux *uhruh* f: heureuse *uhruhz*
hard dur(e) *dewr*
hare le lièvre *lee-aivr*
hat le chapeau *sha-po*
to hate détester *daitestai,* **or (a lot)** avoir horreur de *avwar oruhr duh*
to have avoir *avwar* **(see Verbs p.44), or (a meal, a drink)** prendre *prondr***; to have to** devoir *duhvwar*
hayfever le rhume des foins *rewm dai fwan*
he il *eel*
head la tête *tett* **(see also 'to ache' picture)**
health la santé *sontai;* **health foods** les produits diététiques *prodwee dee-aitai-teek*
healthy (food) sain(e) *san f: senn,* **or (person)** en bonne santé *on bonn sontai*
to hear entendre *ontondr;*
to hear about entendre parler de *ontondr parlai duh*
heart le coeur *kuhr;*
to be heart-broken avoir le coeur brisé *avwar luh kuhr breezai*
heating le chauffage *sho-faj*
heavy lourd(e) *loor f: loord*
helicopter l'hélicoptère [m] *aileekoptair*
hell l'enfer [m] *onfair*
hello bonjour *bonjoor,* **or** salut* *sa-lew*
helmet le casque *kask*
help l'aide [f] *ed;* **help!** au secours! *o suhkoor*

hair les cheveux

to help aider *aidai;* **to help yourself** se servir *suh sairveer*
her (as in "her bag") son *son* f: sa *sa* pl: ses *sai,* **or (as in "it's her" and after "of", "to", "with", etc.)** elle *el,* **or (as in "I see her")** la *la*
here ici *ee-see;* **here is/are** voici *vwa-see*
hi salut* *sa-lew*
hiccups le hoquet *o-kai*
to hide (something) cacher *kashai,* **or (yourself)** se cacher *suh kashai*
hi-fi (system) la chaîne (hi-fi) *shenn (ee-fee)*
high haut(e) *o f: ote*
hiking: to go hiking faire une randonnée *fair ewnn rondonnai*
hill la colline *koleenn*
him (as in "it's him" and after "of", "than", "to", "with", etc.) lui *lwee,* **or (as in "I see/know him")** le *luh*
Hindu hindou(e) *andoo*
hippie le/la hippie *eepee,* **or** le/la bab *bab*
his (as in "his bike") son *son* f: sa *sa* pl: ses *sai*
history l'histoire [f] *eestwar*
hit (success) le succès *sewk-sai,* **or (song)** le tube* *tewb*
to hit (strike) frapper *frappai,* **or (knock into)** heurter *uhrtai*
to hitch (a ride) faire du stop* *fair dew stop*
hitch-hiker l'auto-stoppeur *oto-stopuhr* f: l'auto-stoppeuse *oto-stopuhz*
HIV positive séropositif *sairo-pozeeteef* f: séropositive *sairo-pozeeteev*
hobby le hobby *o-bee*
to hold tenir *tuhneer*
hole le trou *troo*
holiday les vacances [f] *vakonss,* **or (bank holiday)** le jour férié *joor fair-yai;*
holiday camp le camp de vacances *kom duh vakonss*
home la maison *maizon;* **home game** le match à domicile *match a domeesseel;* **at (my/your etc.) home** chez moi/toi *shai mwa/twa*
homeless (people) les sans-abri [m/f] *son-zabree,* **or** le/la SDF *ess dai eff*
homework les devoirs [m] *duhvwar*
homosexual homosexuel(le) *o-mosseksewell,* **or** homo*
honest (law-abiding) honnête *o-net,* **or (truthful)** sincère *sansair*
honey le miel *mee-ell*
to hope espérer *aispairai*
horn (of car) le klaxon *klakson*
horoscope l'horoscope [m] *oroskop* **(see picture below)**
horrible horrible *oreebl*
horror film le film d'épouvante *feelm day-poo-vont*
horse le cheval *shuhval*
hospital l'hôpital [m] *opeetal*
host l'hôte [m] *ote*
hostess l'hôtesse [f] *otess*
hot chaud(e) *sho f: shode,* **or (spicy)** épicé(e) *ai-peessai;* **to be hot (person)** avoir chaud *avwar sho,* **or (weather) it is hot** il fait chaud *eel fai sho*
hotel l'hôtel [m] *otel*
hour l'heure [f] *uhr*
(see also 'time' picture)
house la maison *maizon*
hovercraft l'aéroglisseur [m] *a-airogleessuhr*
how comment *kommon;* **how are you?** comment vas-tu?/allez-vous? *kommon-va-tew/talai-voo;* **how many/much?** combien? *kombee-an*
to hug (someone) serrer (quelqu'un) dans ses bras *sairai (kelkun) don sai bra*
human humain(e) *ew-man f: ew-menn;* **human rights** les droits de l'homme [m] *drwa duh lomm*
humour l'humour [m] *ew-moor*

horoscope
l'horoscope

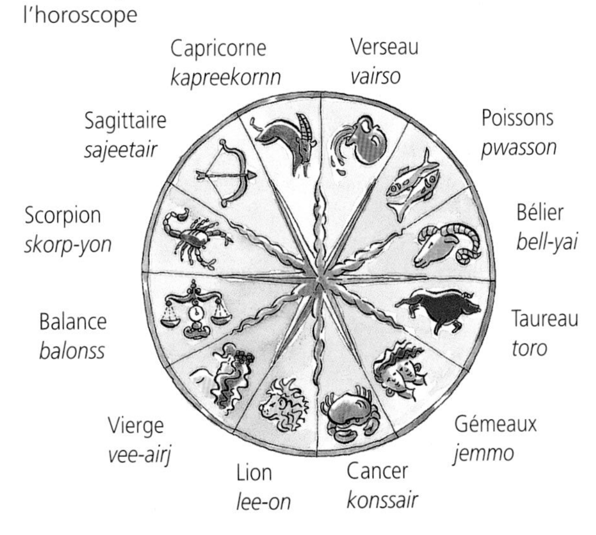

hungry: to be hungry avoir faim *avwar fan*
hurry: in a hurry pressé(e) *praissai*
to hurry se dépêcher *suh daipaishai*
to hurt faire mal *fair mal* (see also 'to ache')
hypocrite l'hypocrite [m/f] *eepokreet*
hysterics (nervous fit) la crise de nerfs *kreez duh nair,* **or (laughter)** le fou rire *foo reer*

I je *juh*
ice la glace *glass;* **ice cream** la glace; **ice cube** le glaçon *gla-sson;* **ice rink** la patinoire *patee-nwar*
idea l'idée [f] *eedai*
idiot l'idiot(e) [m/f] *eed-yo f: eed-yott*
if si *see*
ill malade *malad*
illegal illégal(e) *ee-laigal*
to imagine imaginer *ee-majee-nai*
immigrant l'immigré(e) [m/f] *ee-meegrai*
important important(e) *amporton f: amportont*
in dans *don,* **or (with months, years and [f] names of countries)** en *on,* **e.g. in June** en juin, **in France** en France, **or (with town names and [m] and [pl] names of countries)** à *a,* **e.g. in Paris** à Paris, **in the US** aux États-Unis**; to be in (at home)** être là *etr la;* **the in thing** le must*, **or** le top*
inclusive (tout) compris *(too) kompree*
independent indépendant(e) *andaipondon f: andaipondont*
India l'Inde [f] *and*
infection l'infection [f] *anfekss-yon*
information les renseignements [m] *ronsainn-yuhmon*
injection la piqûre *peekewr*
injury la blessure *blaissewr;* **injury time (in sports)** les arrêts de jeu [m] *arrai duh juh*
innocent innocent(e) *ee-nosson f: ee-nossont*
insect l'insecte [m] *ansekt;* **insect bite** la piqûre d'insecte *peekewr dansekt;* **insect repellent** le produit anti-insectes *prodwee ontee ansekt*
inside à l'intérieur *a lantair-yuhr;* **inside out** à l'envers *a lonvair*
to insist insister *ansseestai*
instead of au lieu de *o lee-uh duh*
instructor le professeur *professuhr,* **or (ski, driving)** le moniteur *monneetuhr* f: la monitrice *monneetreess*
instrument l'instrument [m] *anstrew-mon* **(see also picture on the right)**
insult l'insulte [f] *assewlt*
insurance l'assurance [f] *assewronss*
intercom l'interphone [m] *antairfonn*
interested: to be interested in s'intéresser à *santairaissai a*
interesting intéressant(e) *antairaisson f: antairaissont*
international international(e) *antair-nass-yonnal*
internet internet *internet* **or** le Net *net*
interval (theatre) l'entracte [m] *ontrakt*
interview (for job) l'entretien [m] *ontr-tee-an,* **or (with reporter)** l'interview [f] *antairvew*
to introduce (to person) présenter *praizontai*
invitation l'invitation [f] *anveetass-yon*
to invite inviter *anveetai*
Ireland l'Irlande [f] *eerlond*
Irish irlandais(e) *eerlon-dai f: eerlon-daiz*
island l'île [f] *eel*
it (referring to a [m] thing) il *eel,* **or (referring to a [f] thing)** elle *el,* **or (when unclear what "it" refers to)** ça *sa;* **it is** c'est *sai*
Italy l'Italie [f] *eetalee*

jacket la veste *vest,* **or (short, bomber-style)** le blouson *bloozon* **(see picture on opposite page)**
jam la confiture *konfeetewr*
January janvier *jonvee-ai*

instruments

les instruments
(see also band picture)

jazz le jazz *jazz*
jealous jaloux *jaloo* f: jalouse *jalooz*
jeans le (blue-)jean *(bloo-) djeen*
jellyfish la méduse *maidewz*
jewellery les bijoux [m] *beejoo* (see picture on the right)
Jewish juif *jweef* f: juive *jweev*
job le travail *trav-eye,* **or** le boulot* *boolo,* **or** le job* *djob,* **or (weekend, vacation)** le petit boulot* *puhtee boolo*
to join (club, party) s'inscrire à *sanskreer a*
joke la plaisanterie *plaizontree,* **or** la blague *blag*
to joke plaisanter *plaizontai,* or blaguer* *blagai*
judo le judo *jewdo*
to juggle jongler *jonglai*
juice le jus *jew*
jukebox le juke-box *jewk-boks*
July juillet *jwee-yai*
to jump sauter *so-tai*
June juin *jwan*
junk le bric-à-brac *bree-ka-brak;* **junk shop** le brocanteur *brokontuhr*
just: to have just done (something) venir de faire *vuhneer duh fair*

jacket la veste

jewellery les bijoux

to keep garder *gardai,* **or (not to stop)** ne pas arrêter de *nuh pa-zaraitai duh;* **to keep an eye on** surveiller *sewrvai-yai*
key la clé *klai*
keyboard le clavier *klavyai*
kick le coup de pied *koo duh pee-ai*
kid le/la gamin(e) *ga-man f: ga-meenn,* **or** le/la gosse* *goss*
to kill tuer *tewai;* **to kill yourself (laughing)** être mort(e) de rire *etr mor duh reer f: ...mort...*
kilo le kilo *keelo*
kilometre le kilomètre *keelomaitr*
kind (nice) gentil(le) *jontee f: jonteey*
kiss le baiser *baizai,* **or** la bise *beez,* **or** le bisou *beezoo*
to kiss embrasser *ombrassai,* **or (one another)** s'embrasser *sombrassai*
kit (equipment) le matériel *matair-yell*
kitchen la cuisine *kweezeenn*
kite le cerf-volant *sair volon* (see also picture on p.22)
knee le genou *juh-noo*
knickers le slip *sleep*
knife le couteau *kooto*
to know (facts) savoir *savwar,* **or (person, place)** connaître *konnaitr*
kosher kascher *kashair*

lager la bière (blonde) *bee-air (blond)*
laid-back décontracté(e) *daikontraktai*
lake le lac *lak*
lamb l'agneau [m] *ann-yo*
land la terre *tair*
language la langue *long*
laptop un ordinateur portable *ordee-natuhr portabl*
laser le laser *lazair*
last le dernier *dairnn-yai* f: la dernière *dairnn-yair;* **at last** enfin *onfan*
late (not early) tard *tar,* **or (not on time)** en retard *on ruhtar*
to laugh rire *reer,* **or** rigoler* *reegolai;* **to have a laugh** se marrer* *suh marai;* **to laugh at (a person, thing)** se moquer de *suh mokai duh;* **to burst out laughing** éclater de rire *aiklatai duh reer*

kite le cerf-volant

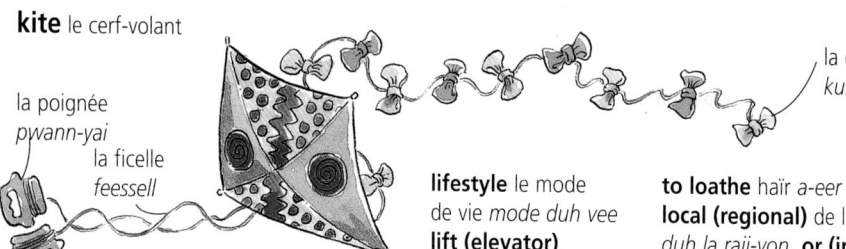

la poignée *pwann-yai*

la ficelle *feessell*

la queue *kuh*

launderette la laverie *lavree*
lazy paresseux *paraissuh* f: paresseuse *paraissuhz*
leaf la feuille *fuh-yuh*
to learn apprendre *aprondr*
leather le cuir *kweer*
to leave laisser *laissai,* **or (go away)** partir *parteer;* **to leave alone** laisser tranquille *laissai tronkeel*
left la gauche *goshe;* **on the left** à gauche; **left-handed** gaucher *go-shai* f: gauchère *go-shair*
leg la jambe *jomb*
lemon le citron *seetron*
to lend prêter *praitai*
leotard le collant *kollon*
less moins *mwan*
lesson le cours *koor*
letter la lettre *letr*
lettuce la salade verte *sa-lad vairt*
liar le menteur *montuhr* f: la menteuse *montuhz*
library la bibliothèque *beeblee-otek*
licence le permis *pairmee;* **driving licence** le permis de conduire *pairmee duh kondweer*
lie (fib) le mensonge *monsonj*
to lie (fib) mentir *monteer*
life la vie *vee*
lifeguard le/la surveillant(e) de baignade *sewrvai-yon duh bainn-yad f: sewrvai-yont...*
lifejacket le gilet de sauvetage *jeelai duh sovtaj*
lifestyle le mode de vie *mode duh vee*
lift (elevator) l'ascenseur [m] *assonsuhr*
light (electric or not darkness) la lumière *lew-mee-air,* **or (not dark)** clair(e) *klair,* **or (not heavy)** léger *laijai* f: légère *laijair*
lighter le briquet *breekai*
like comme *komm;* **what's he/she like?** il/elle est comment? *eel/el ai kommon*
to like aimer *aimmai;* **I like him/her** je l'aime bien *juh laimm bee-an;* **I'd like** je voudrais *juh voodrai,* **or** j'aimerais *jaimm-rai*
likely probable *probabl;* **not likely!** pas question! *pa kesst-yon*
lilac lilas *lee-la*
lilo le matelas pneumatique *matela pnuh-mateek*
line la ligne *leenn-yuh*
lip la lèvre *laivr*
to listen écouter *aikootai*
litre le litre *leetr*
little (small) petit *puhtee* f: petite *puhteet;* **a little (of)** un peu (de) *un puh duh*
live (broadcast) en direct *on deerekt*
to live vivre *veevr,* **or (dwell)** habiter *abeetai;* **to live it up** mener la grande vie *muhnnai la grond vee*
liver le foie *fwa*
living room le salon *salon*
loaded (with money) bourré(e) de fric** *boorai duh freek*
loads of des tas de *dai ta duh*
to loathe haïr *a-eer*
local (regional) de la région *duh la raij-yon,* **or (in/from this part of town)** du quartier *dew kartee-ai,* **or** du coin* *dew kwan*
to lock fermer à clé *fairmai a klai*
London Londres *londr*
lonely seul(e) *surl*
long long(ue) *lon f: long,* **or (a long time)** longtemps *lonton;* **how long? (time)** combien de temps? *kombee-an duh ton*
loo (see 'toilet')
to look regarder *ruhgardai;* **to look after (care for)** soigner *swannyai* **or (take charge of)** s'occuper de *sokewpai duh;* **to look for** chercher *shairshai;* **to look forward to** attendre avec impatience *atondr avek ampass-yonss;* **to look like** ressembler à *ruhssomblai a*
to lose perdre *pairdr*
lost perdu(e) *pairdew;* **to get lost** se perdre *suh pairdr;* **get lost! (clear off!)** fiche le camp* *feesh luh kon* **or** fous le camp** *foo luh kon;* **lost property** les objets trouvés [m] *objai troovai*
lots (a lot) beaucoup *bo-koo,* **or** plein* *plan*
loud fort(e) *for f: fort*
lousy nul(le) *newl*
love l'amour [m] *a-moor;* **in love** amoureux *a-mooruh* f: amoureuse *a-mooruhz;* **love-life** les amours *a-moor*
to love aimer *aimai,* **or (adore)** adorer *adorai*

lovely (pretty) joli(e) *jo-lee,* **or (nice, sweet)** mignon(ne) *meenn-yon f: meenn-yonn*
low bas(se) *ba f: bass;* **low-cut** décolleté(e) *daikoltai*
low-down: to get the low-down (on something) se faire tuyauter* *suh fair twee-yotai*
luck la chance *shonss*; **bad luck** pas de chance *pa duh shonss;* **good luck!** bonne chance! *bonn shonss*
luckily heureusement *uhruhz-mon*
luggage les bagages [m] *bagaj;* **hand-luggage** les bagages à main *bagaj a man*
lunch le déjeuner *daijuh-nai;* **to have lunch** déjeuner *daijuh-nai*
lyrics les paroles [f] *parol*

machine la machine *masheenn*
macho macho* *matcho*
mad fou *foo* f: folle *fol* **(see also 'crazy')**
madam madame *ma-damm*
magazine le magazine *magazeenn*
maggot l'asticot [m] *ass-tee-ko*
mail (letters) le courrier *koor-yai* **(see also 'e-mail')**
to make faire *fair* (see Verbs p.45), **or (earn)** gagner *gann-yai,* **or (as in "it makes me ill/jealous/happy")** rendre *rondr;* **to make up (invent)** inventer *anvontai,* **or (be friends again)** se réconcilier *suh raikonseel-yai*
make-up le maquillage *ma-kee-yaj* (see also picture to the right)
man l'homme [m] *omm*
to manage (cope) se débrouiller *suh daibroo-yai;* **to manage to (succeed)** arriver à *areevai a*
many beaucoup de *bo-koo duh;* **not many** pas beaucoup de *pa bo-koo duh*
map la carte *kart,* **or (of town)** le plan *plon*
March mars *marss*
margarine la margarine *margareenn*
mark (stain) la tache *tash,* **or (at school)** la note *not*
market le marché *marshai*
match (for a candle) l'allumette [f] *alewmett,* **or (sport)** le match *match*
material (cloth) le tissu *teessew*
maths les maths [f] *matt*
matter: it doesn't matter ça ne fait rien *sa nuh fai ree-an;* **what's the matter?** qu'est-ce qui se passe? *kess-kee-suh pass*
mature mûr(e) *mewr*
May mai *mai*
mayonnaise la mayonnaise *my-o-naiz*
me (as in "it's me" and after "of", "than", "to", "with", etc.) moi *mwa,* **or (as in "he sees/knows me")** me *muh*
meal le repas *reh-pa*
to mean vouloir dire *voolwar deer;* **to mean to** avoir l'intention de *avwar lantonss-yon duh*
meat la viande *vee-ond*
media (TV, radio, papers) les médias [m] *maid-ya*
medicine (medication) le médicament *maideekamon,* **or (science)** la médecine *maidseenn*
Mediterranean (sea) la Méditerranée *maideetairannai*
medium (size) moyen(ne) *mwa-yan f: mwa-yenn,* **or (cooking)** à point *a pwan*
to meet (by chance) rencontrer *ronkontrai,* **or (by arrangement)** retrouver *ruhtroovai*
melon le melon *muhlon;* **watermelon** la pastèque *pastek*

make-up le maquillage

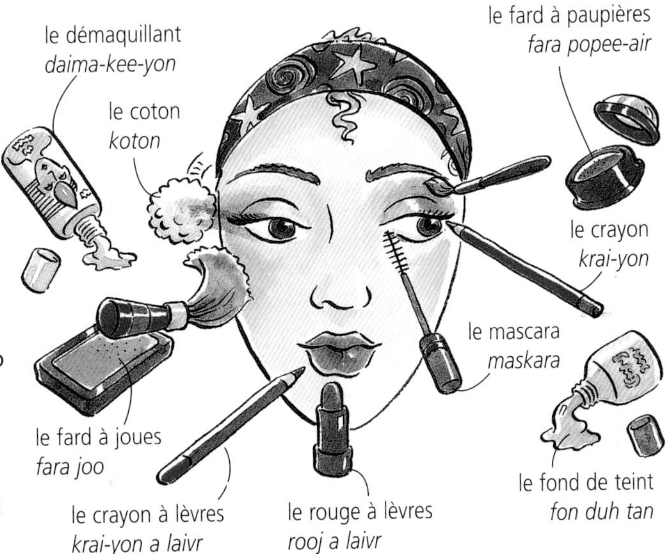

menu la carte *kart,* **or (set menu)** le menu *muh-new*
mess le désordre *daizordr,* **or** la pagaille* *pag-eye*
message le message *messaj*
method la méthode *mai-tod*
metre le mètre *maitr*
microwave le micro-ondes *meekro-ond*
middle le milieu *meel-yuh;* **in the middle (of)** au milieu (de)
midnight minuit *meenn-wee*
milk le lait *lai;* **milk shake** le milk-shake *meelk shaik*
mind: do you mind? **(does it bother you?)** ça te/vous dérange? *sa tuh/voo daironj;* **I don't mind (it doesn't bother me)** ça ne me dérange pas *sa nuh muh daironj pa,* **or (it's all the same to me)** ça m'est égal *sa mai-tai-gal*
minute (time) la minute *mee-newt*
mirror le miroir *meerwar*
Miss mademoiselle *mad-mwazel*
to miss (as in "I missed the train") rater *ratai,* **or (to long for: in French you say "something is missing to you")** manquer *monkai,* **e.g. I miss you** tu me manques, **he misses Paris** Paris lui manque
mistake l'erreur [f] *eruhr;* **to make a mistake** se tromper *suh trompai*
to mix (or to mix up) mélanger *mailonjai,* **or (muddle)** s'embrouiller *sombroo-yai*
mixed up (in your mind) perturbé(e) *pairtewrbai*
to moan (complain) râler* *ralai*
mobile (phone) le mobile *mobeel,* **or** le (téléphone) portable *(tai-lai-fonn) portabl*
model (fashion) le mannequin *mann-kan*
modern moderne *modairnn*
moment: in a moment dans un instant *donzun nanston;* **at the moment** en ce moment *on suh mommon*
Monday lundi [m] *lundee*
money l'argent [m] *arjon,* **or** le fric* *freek;* **money belt** la ceinture porte-billets *santewr port bee-yai*
month le mois *mwa*
monument le monument *monnew-mon*
mood: in a good/bad mood de bonne/mauvaise humeur *duh bonn/movaiz ew-muhr*
moody (temperament) lunatique *lewnnateek*
moon la lune *lewnn*
moped la mobylette *mobeelett*
more (as in "more handsome" and "more slowly") plus *plew,* **or (as in "I want more" and "I like it more")** plus *plewss,* **or (as in "[some] more?")** encore *onkor*
morning le matin *matan*
mosque la mosquée *moskai*
mosquito le moustique *moosteek;* **mosquito bite** la piqûre de moustique *peekewr duh moosteek;* **mosquito repellent** l'anti-moustique [m] *ontee-moosteek*
most (as in "most handsome") le/la/les plus *luh/la/lai plew,* **or (as in "I want the most" and "I like it the most")** le plus *luh plewss,* **or (as in "most of the time/people")** la plupart de *la plewpar duh;* **to make the most of** profiter de *profeetai duh*
mother la mère *mair*
motor le moteur *motuhr*
motorbike la moto* *moto,* **or** la bécane* *baikann*
motorway l'autoroute [f] *otoroot*
mountain la montagne *montann-yuh*
mouse (animal/computer) la souris *soo-ree*
mouth la bouche *boosh*
to move bouger *boojai,* **or (change address)** déménager *daimai-najai;* **move over!** pousse-toi! *pooss twa*
movie le film *feelmm*
movies le cinéma *see-naima,* **or** le ciné*, **or** le cinoche* *see-nosh*
Mr monsieur *muhss-yuh*
Mrs madame *madamm*
much beaucoup *bo-koo*
mugged: to get mugged se faire agresser *suh fair agraissai*
murder le meurtre *murtr*
muscle le muscle *mewsskl*
museum le musée *mewzai*
mushroom le champignon *shompeenn-yon*
music la musique *mewzeek*
musician le/la musicien(ne) *mewzeess-yan* f: *mewzeess-yenn*
Muslim musulman(e) *mewzewlmon f: mewzewlmann*
must (to have to) devoir *duhvwar;* **I must** je dois *juh dwa*
mustard la moutarde *mootard*
my mon *mon* f: ma *ma* pl: mes *mai*

naïve naïf *na-eef* f: naïve *na-eev*
naked nu(e) *new*

name le nom *nom;* **first name** le prénom *prai-nom;* **last name** le nom de famille *nom duh fameey;* **what's your name?** comment tu t'appelles/ vous vous appelez? *komon tew ta-pell/voo voo-za-puhlai*
napkin la serviette *sairvee-ett*
narrow étroit(e) *aitrwa f: aitrwatt*
nasty désagréable *daizagrai-abl,* **or (person, animal)** méchant(e) *maishon f: maishont*
national national(e) *nass-yonnal*
nationality la nationalité *nass-yonnaleetai*
natural naturel(le) *natewrel*
nature la nature *natewr*
naughty vilain(e) *veelan f: veelenn*
near près de *prai duh*
nearest le/la plus proche *plew prosh*
nearly presque *presk*
necessary nécessaire *naissaissair*
neck le cou *koo*
to need avoir besoin de *avwar buhzwan duh*
needle l'aiguille [f] *aigweey*
neighbour le/la voisin(e) *vwazan f: vwazeenn*
neighbourhood le quartier *kart-yai*
nerve le nerf *nair;* **nerve-racking** angoissant(e) *ong-wasson f: ong-wassont;* **to get on (someone's) nerves** taper sur les nerfs* (de quelqu'un) *ta-pai sewr lai nairf (duh kelkun);* **what a nerve!** quel culot!* *kel kewlo*
nervous: to be/feel nervous être tendu(e) *etr tondew,* **or (have butterflies)** avoir le trac* *avwar luh trak*
never jamais *jammai;* **never mind! (it doesn't matter)** ça ne fait rien! *sa nuh fai ree-an,* **or (too bad)** tant pis! *ton pee*
new nouveau† *noo-vo* f: nouvelle *noo-vel;* **New Year** le nouvel an *noo-vel on;*
New Zealand la Nouvelle-Zélande *noo-vel zailond*
news les nouvelles [f] *noo-vel,* **or (TV, radio, press)** les informations [f] *anformass-yon,* **or** les infos* *anfo;* **news stand** le kiosque *kee-osk* **newsagent's (for papers)** le marchand de journaux *marshon duh joorno,* **or (for cigarettes)** le tabac *taba*
newspaper le journal *joornal*
next prochain(e) *proshan f: proshenn;* **next to** à côté de *a kotai duh*
nice (likeable) sympa* *sampa;* **nice and... (as in "nice and cold")** bien *bee-an*
nickname le surnom *sewr-nom,* **or (shortened name)** le diminutif *dee-mee-newteef*
night la nuit *nwee;* **last night** hier soir *ee-air swar*
nightmare le cauchemar *koshmar*
no non *non;* **no entry/smoking** défense d'entrer/de fumer *daifonss dontrai/duh fewmai;* **no way!** pas question! *pa kesst-yon*
nobody personne *pairsonn;* **nobody else** personne d'autre *pairsonn dotr*
noise le bruit *brwee*
normal normal(e) *nor-mal*
north le nord *nor;* **north of** au nord de *o nor duh*
nose *le nez nai*
nosy curieux *kewr-yuh* f: curieuse *kewr-yuhz;* **to be nosy** fourrer son nez partout* *foorai son nai partoo*
not (with a verb, as in "it's not working") ne... pas *nuh... pa,* **or (without a verb, as in "not me")** pas *pa*
note (money) le billet *bee-yai*
notebook le carnet *karnai*
nothing rien *ree-an;* **nothing else** rien d'autre *ree-an dotr*
novel le roman *rommon*
November novembre *novombr*
now maintenant *mant-non*
nowhere nulle part *newl par*
nuclear nucléaire *newklai-air*
number le numéro *new-mairo*
nurse l'infirmier *anfeerm-yai* f: l'infirmière *anfeerm-yair*
nuts les noix [f] *nwa* **(see picture on p.26)**
nutter (crazy person) le fou *foo* f: la folle *fol,* **or** le/la cinglé(e)** *sanglai*

obnoxious odieux *od-yuh* f: odieuse *od-yuhz*
obscene obscène *obsenn*
obsession l'obsession [f] *obsaiss-yon*
obvious évident(e) *aiveedon f: aiveedont*
o'clock (see picture for 'time')
October octobre *oktobr*
odd (strange) bizarre *beezar;* **the odd one out** l'exception [f] *eksepss-yon*
of de *duh* **(see p.45)**
off (switched off) éteint(e) *aitan f: aitant;* **(see also to get, to put, to take, to turn, etc.)**
offended vexé(e) *veksai*
to offer offrir *offreer*
office le bureau *bewro*
official officiel(le) *ofeess-yell*

†**nouveau** changes to **nouvel** *noovell* in front of a [m] word beginning with a vowel or sometimes an "h".

often souvent *soovon;* **how often?** combien de fois? *kombee-an duh fwa*
oil l'huile [f] *weel*
OK d'accord *da-kor,* **or** OK*, **or (I'm/it's OK)** ça va *sa va*
old vieux† *vee-uh* f: vieille *vee-aiy;* **how old are you?** quel âge as-tu? *kel aj a tew;*
old-fashioned démodé(e) *dai-modai,* **or** ringard(e)* *rangar f: rangard*
olive l'olive [f] *oleev*
omelette l'omelette [f] *omm-lett*
on sur *sewr,* **or (switched on)** allumé(e) *alew-mai;* **on Sundays** le dimanche *luh dee-monsh;* **to be on (as in "where's the film on?")** passer *passai*
one-way à sens unique *a sonss ew-neek*
onion l'oignon [m] *onn-yon*
only seulement *surlmon;* **only daughter/son** la fille/le fils unique *feey/feess ew-neek*
open ouvert(e) *oovair f: oovairt;* **in the open air** en plein air *on plenn-air*
to open ouvrir *oovreer*
opera l'opéra [m] *opaira*
opinion l'avis [m] *avee*
opportunity l'occasion [f] *okaz-yon*
opposite (facing) en face *on fass,* **or (not the same)** le contraire *kontrair*
optician's chez l'opticien(ne) [m/f] *shai lopteess-yan f: ...lopteess-yen*
optimistic optimiste *optee-meest*
or ou *oo*
orange (fruit) l'orange [f] *oronj,* **or (colour)** orange
orchestra l'orchestre [m] *orkestr*
order l'ordre [m] *ordr,* **or (for food, drink)** la commande *kommond*
to order (food, drink) commander *kommondai*
ordinary ordinaire *ordee-nair*
organic (produce) produit biologique *prod-wee bee-olojeek* **or** bio* *bee-o*
to organize organiser *organneezai*
original original(e) *oreejeennal*
other autre *otr;* **the other one** l'autre [m/f]
otherwise sinon *see-non*
our notre *notr* pl: nos *no*
out: to be out (not at home) être sorti(e) *etr sortee;*
out of order (not working) en panne *on pann* **(see also to find, to go, etc.)**
outdoor de plein air *duh plenn-air;* **to sleep outdoors** dormir à la belle étoile *dormeer a la bel aitwal*
outrageous monstrueux *monss-trew-uh* f: monstrueuse *monss-trew-uhz*
outside à l'extérieur *a lex-tair-yuhr,* **or** dehors *duh-or*
oven le four *foor*
over (not under) par-dessus *par duhssew,* **or (finished)** fini(e) *fee-nee;* **over here** par ici *par ee-see;* **over there** là-bas *la-ba;* **over the top** exagéré(e) *egzajairai*
overdraft le découvert *daikoovair*
overrated surestimé(e) *sewr-esstee-mai*

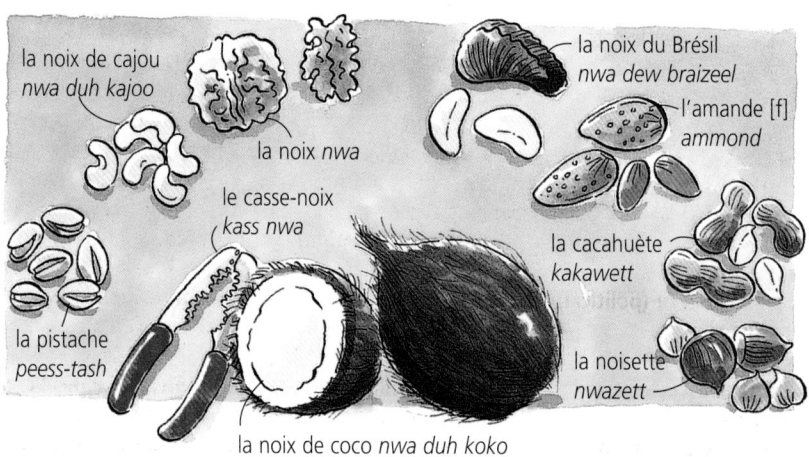

nuts les noix

†***vieux*** changes to ***vieil*** *(vee-ai)* in front of a [m] word beginning with a vowel and sometimes "h", e.g. ***un vieil homme***.

to overtake doubler *dooblai*
to owe devoir *duhvwar*
own: on your own tout(e) seul(e) *too surl f: toot surl*
owner le/la propriétaire *propree-aitair*

to pack (bags) faire les valises *fair lai valeez*
package tour le voyage organisé *vwa-yaj organneezai*
padlock le cadenas *kad-na,* **or (on bike)** l'antivol [m] *onteevol*
page la page *paj*
pain: to be a pain (nuisance) être embêtant(e) *etr ombaiton f: ombaitont*
to paint peindre *pandr*
painting la peinture pantoor
palace le palais *palai*
pan (saucepan) la casserole *kass-rol,* **or (frying)** la poêle *pwal*
panic la panique *panneek*
paper le papier *pap-yai*
paperback (book) le livre de poche *leevr duh posh*
parachute le parachute *parashewt*
parcel le colis *kolee*
parents les parents [m] *pa-ron*
park le jardin public *jardan pewbleek,* **or (large)** le parc *park*
to park se garer *suh ga-rai*
parking space le parking *parkeeng*
part (not all) la partie *partee,* **or (for bike etc.)** la pièce *pee-ess;* **to take part** participer *parteesseepai*
party la fête *fett,* **or (political)** le parti *partee*
to party faire la fête *fair la fett*
pass (for travel) la carte (d'abonnement) *kart (dabonn-mon);* **ski pass** le forfait *forfai*
to pass passer *passai,* **or (exam)** réussir *rai-ewsseer*
passenger le passager *passajai* f: la passagère *passajair*
passport le passeport *passpor*
pasta les pâtes [f] *patt*
path le chemin *shuh-man*
patient patient(e) *pass-yon f: pass-yont*
pattern le motif *moteef*
pavement le trottoir *trotwar*
to pay payer *pai-yai;* **to pay back** rembourser *romboorsai*
peace la paix *pai*
peaceful tranquille *tronkeel*
peach la pêche *pesh*
peanut la cacahuète *kakawett*
pear la poire *pwar*
peas les petits pois [m] *puhtee pwa*
pedestrian le piéton *pee-aiton;* **pedestrian crossing** le passage (pour) piétons *passaj (poor) pee-aiton*
to peel éplucher *ai-plooshai*
pen le stylo *steelo;* **pen pal** le/la correspondant(e) *ko-respondon f: ko-respondont*
pencil le crayon *krai-yon*
people les gens [m/f] *jon*
pepper (spice) le poivre *pwavr*, **or (vegetable)** le poivron *pwavron*
perfect parfait(e) *parfai f: parfett*
performance la représentation *ruhprai-zontass-yon,* **or (cinema)** la séance *sai-onss*
perhaps peut-être *puh-tetr*
period (menstruation) les règles [f] *raigl*
person la personne *pairsonn*
petrol l'essence [f] *essonss;* **lead-free petrol** le sans plomb *son plom;* **petrol station** la station-service *stass-yon sairveess*
pharmacy la pharmacie *farmassee*
philosophy la philosophie *feelo-zofee*
phobia la phobie *fobee*
phone le téléphone *tai-lai-fonn;* **phone booth** la cabine téléphonique *ka-beenn tai-lai-fonneek;* **phone call** le coup de fil *koo duh feel* (see also picture on p.28)
to phone téléphoner *tai-lai-fonnai,* **or** passer un coup de fil* *passai un koo duh feel;* **to phone back** rappeler *rap-lai*
photo la photo *foto*
photographer le/la photographe *fotograf*
to pick (choose) choisir *shwazeer,* **or (gather)** cueillir *kuh-yeer;* **to pick up (from floor/table, etc.)** ramasser *rammassai*
picnic le pique-nique *peek neek* (see also picture on p.29)
picture (drawing) le dessin *daissan,* **or (painting)** le tableau *tablo*
pie (meat/vegetable) la tourte *toort,* **or (sweet)** la tarte *tart*
piece le morceau *morso*
pig le cochon *koshon*
pigeon le pigeon *peejon*
pill la pilule *peelewl*
PIN (personal identification number) le code confidentiel *kod konfeedonsee-ell*
pinball le flipper *fleepuhr*
pineapple l'ananas [m] *annannass*
pink rose *roz*
pity: it's a pity! c'est dommage! *sai dommaj*
pizza la pizza *peedza*

phone booth la cabine téléphonique

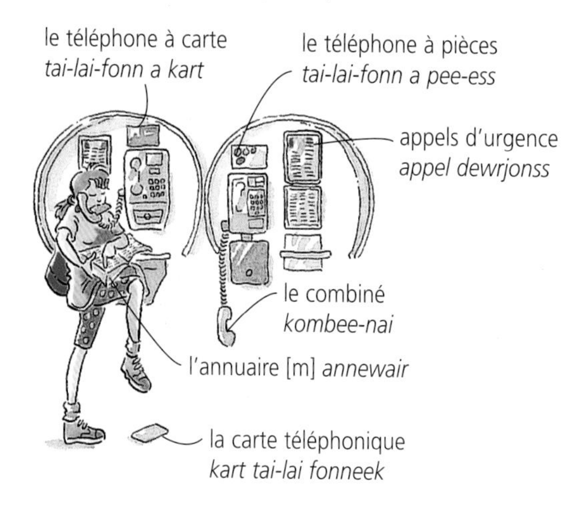

place l'endroit [m] *ondrwa,* **or (seat, position)** la place *plass;* **(at/to) my/your place** chez moi/toi *shai mwa/twa*
plan le plan *plon*
plane (aircraft) l'avion [m] *av-yon*
plant la plante *plont*
plaster (for cut or blister) le pansement *ponss-mon,* **or (cast)** le plâtre *platr*
plastic le plastique *plasteek*
plate l'assiette [f] *ass-yett*
play (in theatre) la pièce *pee-yess*
to play jouer *joo-ai*
player le joueur *joo-uhr* f: la joueuse *joo-uhz*
please s'il vous plaît *seel voo plai,* **or (to a friend)** s'il te plaît *seel tuh plai*
plug (for water) la bonde *bond,* **or (for electrics)** la prise *preez*
plum la prune *prewn*
pocket la poche *posh;* **pocket-money** l'argent de poche [m] *arjon duh posh*
poem le poème *po-emm*
to point indiquer *andeekai,* **or (with a finger)** montrer du doigt *montrai dew dwa*
police la police *poleess;* **police officer** l'agent de police [m] *ajon duh poleess,* **or** le gendarme *jondarm,* **or** le flic* *fleek;* **police station** le commissariat de police *komeess-areea duh poleess*
polite poli(e) *polee*
politics la politique *poleeteek*
pollution la pollution *polewss-yon*
pomegranate la grenade *gren-add*
pond l'étang [m] *ay-tan*
poor pauvre *pohvr*
popular populaire *popewlair*
pork le porc *por*
posh (elegant) chic *sheek*
positive (not negative) positif *pozeeteef* f: positive *pozeeteev,* **or (sure)** sûr(e) *sewr*
possible possible *posseebl*
post (letters) le courrier *kooree-ai;* **post-box** la boîte aux lettres *bwat o letr;* **post office** la poste *post*
postcard la carte postale *kart postal*
poster le poster *postair*
potato la pomme de terre *pomm duh tair;* **mashed potato** la purée (de pomme de terre) *pewrai (duh pomm duh tair)*
pound (UK money) la livre (sterling) *leevr (stairleeng)*
poverty la pauvreté *pohvretai*
practical pratique *prateek*
to practise (sport) s'entraîner *sontrainnai,* **or (piano, violin)** travailler *trav-eye-ai*
prawn la crevette *kruhvett*
to prefer préférer *praifairai*
pregnant enceinte *onsant*
to prepare préparer *praiparai*
present (gift) le cadeau *kado*
to pretend faire semblant *fair somblon*
pretty joli(e) *jolee*
price le prix *pree*
printer (machine) l'imprimante [f] *ampree-mont*
prison la prison *preezon*
private privé(e) *preevai*
prize le prix *pree*
problem le problème *problemm*
product le produit *prodwee*
programme le programme *programm,* **or (TV, radio)** l'émission [f] *ai-meess-yon*
progress le progrès *prograi*
promise la promesse *pro-mess*
proof la preuve *prurv*
Protestant protestant(e) *proteston f: protestont*
proud fier f: fière *fee-air*
psychological psychologique *pseekolojeek*
public public f: publique *pewbleek*

to pull tirer *teerai;* **to pull someone's leg** faire marcher quelqu'un* *fair marshai kelkun*
to punch donner un coup de poing *donnai un koo duh pwan*
puncture: to have a puncture (tyre) avoir (le pneu) crevé *avwar (luh pnuh) kruhvai*
pure pur(e) *pewr*
purpose: on purpose exprès *aiksprai*
purse (for coins) le porte-monnaie *port monnai*
to push pousser *poossai*
to put mettre *metr;* **to put away** ranger *ronjai;* **to put off (postpone)** remettre à plus tard *ruh-metr a plew tar,* **or (discourage)** dissuader *deess-ew-adai,* **or (disgust)** dégoûter *daigootai;* **to put on (clothes)** mettre *metr;* **to put (someone) up** loger *lojai;* **to put up with** supporter *sewportai*
puzzle le puzzle *pewzl*

quality la qualité *ka-leetai*
quantity la quantité *konteetai*
to quarrel se disputer *suh deespewtai*
quarter le quart *kar* (see also time picture)
queen la reine *ren*
question la question *kest-yon*
queue la queue *kuh*
to queue faire la queue *fair la kuh*
quick rapide *rapeed*
quickly vite *veet*
quiet (calm) tranquille *tronkeel,* **or (not loud)** bas *ba* f: basse *bass;* **to be/**
keep quiet se taire *suh tair*
quite (as in "quite pretty") assez *assai,* **or (as in "I quite agree")** tout à fait *too-ta-fai*
quiz le jeu *juh,* **or** le concours *konkoor*
quotation (estimate) le devis *devee*

race la course *koorss*
racist raciste *rasseest*
racket (tennis etc.) la raquette *rakett*
radiator le radiateur *rad-yatuhr*
radio la radio *rad-yo*
raft le radeau *ra-do*
rage la furie *fooree*
railway le chemin de fer *shuh-man duh fair;* **French railways** la SNCF *ess enn sai eff*
rain la pluie *plwee;*
it's raining il pleut *eel pluh* (see picture on p.30)
rare (unusual) rare *rar,* **or (barely cooked)** saignant(e) *senn-yon f:senn-yont*
rash l'irritation [f] *eereetass-yon*
raspberry la framboise *frombwaz*
raw cru(e) *krew*
razor le rasoir *razwar;* **razor blade** la lame de rasoir *lamm duh razwar*
reaction la réaction *rai-aks-yon*
to read lire *leer*
ready prêt(e) *prai f: prait*
real vrai(e) *vrai*
to realize se rendre compte *suh rondr komt*
really (truly, extremely) vraiment *vrai-mon,* **or (extremely)** vachement* *vash-mon*
reason la raison *raizon*
recent récent(e) *raisson f: raissont*

picnic le pique-nique

rain la pluie

l'arc-en-ciel [m]
ar-konss-yell

le parapluie
paraplwee

la flaque d'eau
flak doh

l'imper* [m]
ampair

la goutte de pluie
goot duh plwee

la botte de caoutchouc
bott duh ka-ootchoo

reception la réception *rai-seps-yon*
recipe la recette *ruhsett*
to recognize reconnaître *ruhkonnaitr*
to recommend recommander *ruhkommondai*
record (sport) le record *ruhkor*
to record enregistrer *onruh-jeestrai*
red rouge *rooj;* **to blush** rougir *roojeer* (see also 'hair')
reduced (in sales) soldé(e) *soldai*
refund le remboursement *romboorss-mon*
to refuse refuser *ruhfewzai*
region la région *raij-yon*
registered (post, letter) recommandé(e) *ruhkommondai,* **or (luggage)** enregistré(e) *onruhjeestrai*
regular régulier *raigewl-yai* f: régulière *raigewl-yair*
rehearsal la répétition *raipaiteess-yon*
to relax se détendre *suh daitondr*
relaxed décontracté(e) *daikontraktai*
relief le soulagement *soolaj-mon*
religion la religion *ruhleej-yon*
to relive revivre *ruh-veevr*
to remember se souvenir de *suh soov-neer duh*
remote isolé(e) *eezolai;* **remote control** la télé-commande *tailai-kommond*
to rent louer *loo-ai;* **for rent** à louer
to repair réparer *raiparai*
to repeat répéter *raipaitai*
to reply répondre *raipondr*
rescue les secours [m] *suhkoor*
to rescue sauver *sovai*
research la recherche *ruh-shairsh*
reservation la réservation *raizairvass-yon*
reserved réservé(e) *raizairvai*
responsible responsable *raisponsabl*
rest (break) le repos *ruhpo,* **or (remainder)** le reste *rest*
to rest se reposer *suh ruhpozai*
restaurant le restaurant *restoron,* **or** le resto*
result le résultat *raizewlta*
return le retour *ruhtoor,* **or (ticket)** l'aller-retour [m] *allai ruhtoor*
revenge: to get your revenge se venger *suh vonjai*
to reverse faire marche arrière *fair marsh ar-yair;* **to reverse the charges (phone)** appeler en PCV *appuhlai on pai sai vai*
rice le riz *ree*
rich riche *reesh*
rid: to get rid of se débarrasser de *suh daibarrassai duh*
ride: to go for a ride (bike/ car) faire un tour *fair un toor;* **to take someone for a ride (trick)** faire marcher quelqu'un *fair marshai kelkun*
rider (horse) le cavalier *kaval-yai;* la cavalière *kaval-yair*
riding l'équitation [f] *aikeetass-yon* **(see also picture on the opposite page)**
right (correct) exact *egzakt,* **or (fair)** juste *jewst,* **or (not left)** la droite *drwat;* **you are right** tu as/vous avez raison *tew a/ voo-zavai raizon;* **on the right** à droite*;* **right away** tout de suite *tood sweet;* **right-of-way** la priorité, *pree-oreetai*
to ring sonner *sonnai* **(see also 'phone')**
riot l'émeute [f] *emmurt;* **to have a riot (wild time)** s'éclater** *saiklatai*
to rip déchirer *daisheerai*
ripe mûr(e) *mewr*
rip-off: it's a rip-off c'est de l'arnaque** *sai duh lar-nak*
risk le risque *reesk*
river la rivière *reev-yair,* **or (large)** le fleuve *flurv*
road la route *root,* **or (in town)** la rue *rew;* **road map** la carte routière *kart root-yair*
rock (boulder, rock-face) le rocher *roshai,* **or (music)** le rock *rok*

roll (bread) le petit pain *puhtee pan*
roller blades les rollers (m) *roluhr*
romance (love affair/story) l'histoire d'amour [f] *eestwar da-moor*
romantic romantique *ro-monteek*
roof le toit *twa;* **roof rack** la galerie *galree*
room la pièce *pee-ess,* **or (hotel/bedroom)** la chambre *shombr;* **single/double room** la chambre simple/double *shombr sampl/doobl;* **twin room** la chambre à deux lits *shombr a duh lee*
rope la corde *kord*
rotten (off) pourri(e) *pooree,* **or (mean, unfair)** moche* *mosh*
round (of drinks) la tournée *toor-nai,* **or (shape)** rond(e) *ron f: rond*
roundabout le rond-point *ron-pwan*
route l'itinéraire [m] *eetee-nairair*
to row (a boat) ramer *ramai*
to rub frotter *frotai;* **to rub it in** remuer le couteau dans la plaie *ruhmewai luh kooto don la plai;* **to rub out** effacer *aifassai*
rubber band l'élastique [m] *ailasteek*
rubbish les ordures [f] *ord-ewr;* **rubbish bin** la poubelle *poobel;* **to talk rubbish** dire des bêtises *deer dai baiteez*
rude impoli(e) *ampolee,* **or (crude)** grossier *gross-yai* f: grossière *gross-yair*
rugby le rugby *rewgbee*
ruins les ruines [f] *rween*
rule la règle *raigl*
rumour la rumeur *rewmuhr*
to run courir *kooreer;* **to run away** s'enfuir *sonfweer;* **to run out (expire)** expirer *ekspeerai*
rush hour l'heure de pointe [f] *uhr duh pwant*
sad triste *treest*
safe en sécurité *on saikew-reetai,* **or (for valuables)** le coffre-fort *kofr for*
safety la sécurité *saikewreetai;* **safety belt** la ceinture de sécurité *santewr duh saikewreetai;* **safety pin** épingle de sûreté *aipangl duh sewr-tai*
sailing: sailing boat (yacht) le voilier *vwall-yai,* **or (dinghy)** le dériveur *daireevuhr;* **to go sailing** faire de la voile *fair duh la vwal* **(see also picture on p.32)**
salad la salade *salad;* **fruit salad** la salade de fruits *salad duh frwee;* **green salad** la salade verte *salad vairt;* **mixed salad** la salade composée *salad kompozai;* **salad dressing (French dressing)** la vinaigrette *vee-naigrett*
salami le saucisson *sosseesson*

riding l'équitation

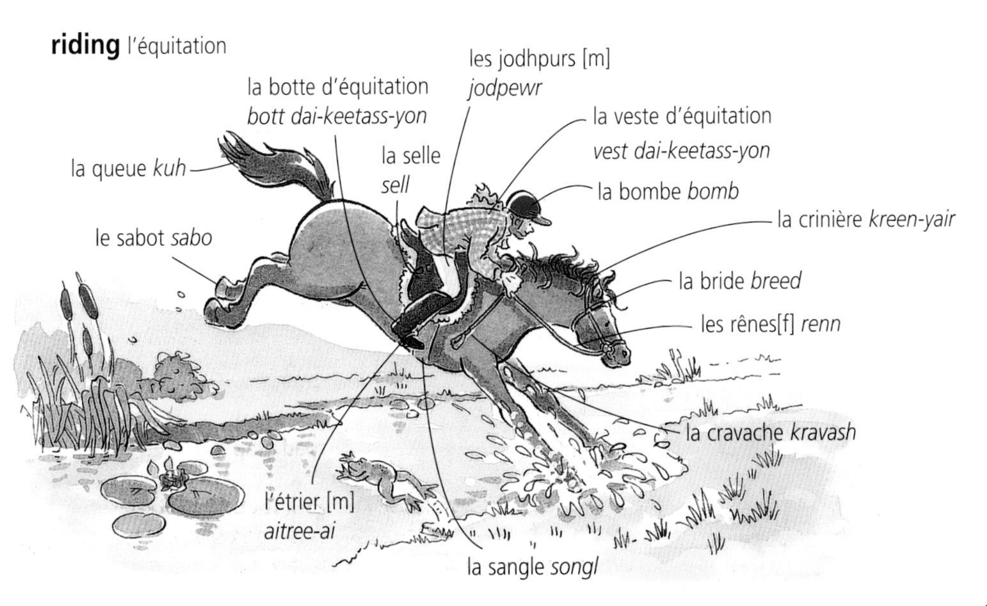

sailing boat le voilier **or** le dériveur

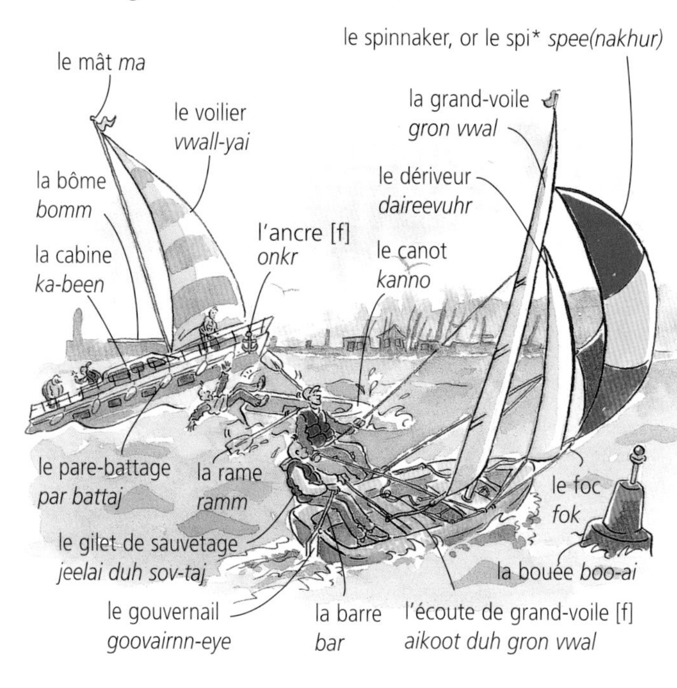

sale: for sale à vendre *a vondr*
sales (reduced prices) les soldes [f] *solld*
salmon le saumon *so-mon*
salt le sel *sell*
salty salé *sall-ai*
same le/la même *memm*
sand le sable *sabl*
sandal la sandale *sondal*
sandwich le sandwich *sondweesh*
sanitary towel la serviette hygiénique *sairv-yett eejai-neek*
sarcastic sarcastique *sarkasteek*
Saturday samedi [m] *sammdee*
sauce la sauce *sosse*
sausage la saucisse *sosseess*
to save (rescue) sauver *sovai,* **or (money)** économiser *aiko-no-meezai*
savoury (not sweet) salé(e) *sa-lai*
to say dire *deer*
scared: to be scared avoir peur *avwar puhr,* **or** avoir la trouille** *avwar la troo-yuh;*
scared stiff mort(e) de peur *mor duh puhr f: mort...*
scarf (long) l'écharpe [f] *aisharp,* **or (square)** le foulard *foolar*
scary effrayant(e) *efrai-yon f: efrai-yont*
scenery le paysage *pai-ee-zaj*
school (primary) l'école [f] *aikol,* **or (high/secondary)** le lycée *lee-sai,* **or** le collège *kolej*
science la science *see-onss*
scissors les ciseaux [m] *seezo*
score le score *skor*
to score (a goal, point) marquer un but/un point *markai un bewt/un pwan*
Scotland l'Écosse [f] *aikoss*
Scottish écossais(e) *aikossai f: aikossaiz*
to scratch (yourself) se gratter *suh gratai*
to scream crier *kree-ai*
screen l'écran [m] *aikron*
scruffy crade** *krad*
sculpture la sculpture *skewl-tewr*
sea la mer *mair*
seafood les fruits de mer [m] *frwee duh mair*
seasick: to be seasick avoir le mal de mer *avwar luh mal duh mair*
season la saison *saizon;*
season ticket la carte d'abonnement *kart dabonn-mon*
seat (place) la place *plass,* **or (chair)** le siège *see-aij*
second (measurement of time) la seconde *suhgond;*
second-hand d'occasion *dokaz-yon*
secret le secret *suhkrai*
secretary le/la secrétaire *suhkraitair*
security la sécurité *say-koo-ree-tai*
to see voir *vwar;* **to see again** revoir *ruhvwar;* **see you soon** à bientôt *a bee-anto*
to seem sembler *somblai*
selfish égoïste *aigo-eest*
self-service (restaurant) le self(-service)* *self(-sairveess)*
to sell vendre *vondr*
to send envoyer *onvwa-yai*
sense le sens *sonss;*
it doesn't make sense ça n'a pas de sens *sa na pa duh sonss*
sensible raisonnable *raizonnabl*
sensitive sensible *sonsseebl*

September septembre *septombr*
serious sérieux *sair-yuh* f: sérieuse *sair-yuhz*
service le service *sairveess*
sewing la couture *kootuhr*
sex (gender) le sexe *seks*
sexist sexiste *sekseest*
sexy sexy *seksy*
shade l'ombre [f] *ombr;* **in the shade** *à l'ombre*
shame la honte *ont;* **what a shame!** (quel) dommage! *kel dommaj*
shampoo le shampooing *shompwan*
shape la forme *form*
to share partager *partajai*
shattered (tired) nase** *naz,* **or** crevé(e)** *kruhvai*
to shave se raser *suh ra-zai*
shaving cream la crème à raser *kremm a ra-zai*
she elle *el*
shell la coquille kok-eel
sheet le drap *dra*
shirt la chemise *shuh-meez*
shock *le choc shok*
shoe la chaussure *sho-sewr,* **or** la pompe** *pomp,* **or** la godasse** *godass;* **athletics shoes** les baskets [f] *baskett*
shop le magasin *magazan,* **or** la boutique *booteek*
shopping: to go shopping (for groceries etc.) faire des courses *fair dai koorss,* **or (for clothes etc.)** faire les magasins *fair lai magazan;* **shopping centre** le centre commercial *sontr kommairsee-al;* **window shopping** le lèche-vitrines *lesh-veetreenn*
short court(e) *koor f: koort;* **short cut** le raccourci *ra-koorsee;* **short-sighted** myope *mee-op*
shorts le short *short*
shoulder l'épaule [f] *aipole*
to shout crier *kree-ai,* **or** hurler *ewrlai*
show (performance) le spectacle *spek-takl*
to show montrer *montrai;* **to show off** frimer** *freemai*
shower la douche *doosh*
shut fermé(e) *fair-mai;* **shut up!** tais-toi! *tai-twa,* **or** taisez-vous *taizai-voo,* **or** ferme-la *fairm-la*
shy timide *tee-meed*
sick (ill) malade *malad;* **to be sick (vomit)** vomir *vo-meer;* **to feel sick (queasy)** avoir mal au coeur *avwar mal o kuhr*
side le côté *kotai*
sightseeing le tourisme *tooreezm*
sign (with hand etc.) le signe *seenn-yuh,* **or (on road etc.)** le panneau *panno*
signature la signature *seenn-yatewr*
Sikh sikh *seek*
silence le silence *seelonss*
silly bête *bet*
simple simple *sampl*
since depuis *duhpwee*
to sing chanter *shontai*
singer le chanteur *shontuhr* f: la chanteuse *shontuhz*
single (ticket) l'aller simple [m] *allai sampl,* **or (unmarried)** célibataire *saileebatair*
Sir Monsieur *muhss-yuh*
sister la soeur *suhr,* **or** la frangine* *fronjeenn*
to sit down s'asseoir *sass-war*
sitting down assis(e) *assee f: asseez*
size la taille *tie*
skate le patin *patan*
skate board la planche à roulettes *plonsh a roolett,* **or** le skate* *skate*
skating: ice-skating le patin (à glace) *patan (a gla-ss);* **roller skating** les rollers (m) *roluhr*
to ski skier *skee-ai*
skiing le ski *skee;* **water-skiing** le ski nautique *skee noteek;* **to go skiing** faire du ski *fair dew skee;* **ski resort** la station de ski *stass-yon duh skee*
(see also picture on p.35)
skin la peau *po*
skirt la jupe *jewp*
skiver le/la tire-au-flanc* *teer-o-flon*
sky le ciel *see-ell*
slang l'argot [m] *argo*
to sleep dormir *dor-meer;* **to sleep in** faire la grasse matinée *fair la grass matee-nai*
sleeper (on train) la couchette *kooshett*
sleeping bag le sac de couchage *sak duh kooshaj*
slice la tranche *tronsh*
to slip glisser *gleessai*
slob le/la plouc** *plook*
slow lent(e) *lon f: lont*
slowly lentement *lont-mon*
sly rusé(e) *rewzai*
small petit(e) *puhtee f: puhteet*
smart (cunning) malin *malan* f: maligne *maleenn,* **or (elegant)** chic *sheek*
smell l'odeur [f] *oduhr*
to smell sentir *sonteer,* **or (stink)** puer *pewai*
smile le sourire *sooreer*
to smile sourire *sooreer*
to smoke fumer *few-mai*
smoking (sign) fumeurs *few-muhr;* **non-smoking** non fumeurs *non-few-muhr*
snack le casse-croûte *kass-kroot*
snail l'escargot *eskargo*
snake le serpent *sairpon*

sneaky (cunning) rusé(e) *rewzai*
to sneeze éternuer *aitair-new-ai*
sniff renifler *ruhneeflai*
snobbish snob *snob*
snore ronfler *ronflai*
snow la neige *nej;*
snowball la boule de neige *bool duh nej* **(see also 'weather')**
so (as in "it's so easy") tellement *tell-mon,* **or** si *see,* **or (as in "so, be quick")** alors *alor;* **so-so (not great)** pas génial(e)* *pa jainn-yal*
soaking (wet) trempé(e) *trompai*
soap le savon *sa-von;*
soap opera le feuilleton *fuh-yuh-ton*
sob sangloter *songlotai*
soccer (football) le football *footbol,* **or** le foot* **(see also football)**
society la société *soss-yaitai*
sock la chaussette *sho-sett*
socket (electrical) la prise *preez*
soft doux *doo* f: douce *dooss,* **or (not firm)** mou *moo* f: molle *mol;* **soft drink** la boisson non alcoolisée *bwasson nonnal-koleezai*
software le logiciel *lojeess-yel*
soldier le soldat *solda*
solid solide *soleed*
some du *dew* f: de la *duh la* pl: des *dai,* **or (as in "some [of them]" and "some people")** certain(e)s *sairtan f: sairtenn*
somebody quelqu'un *kelkun;* **somebody else** quelqu'un d'autre *kelkun dotr*
something quelque chose *kelkuh-shoze;* **something else** quelque chose d'autre *kelkuh-shoze dotr*
sometimes quelquefois *kelkuh-fwa*
somewhere quelque part *kelkuh-par;* **somewhere else** ailleurs *eye-uhr*
song la chanson *shonsson*
soon bientôt *bee-anto*
sorry (excuse me/forgive me) pardon *par-don,* **or (as in "I'm really sorry")** désolé(e) *daizolai*
sort le genre *jonr*
sound le son *son*
soup la soupe *soop,* **or** le potage *potaj*
south le sud *sewd;* **south of** au sud de *o sewd duh*
souvenir le souvenir *soov-neer*
space l'espace [m] *esspass,* **or (room)** la place *plass*
Spain l'Espagne [f] *esspann-yuh*
spare (extra) en trop *on tro;* **spare part** la pièce de rechange *pee-ess duh ruh-shonj;* **spare time** le temps libre *ton leebr,* **or** les loisirs [m] *lwazeer*
to speak parler *parlai*
speaker (loudspeaker) le haut-parleur *o-par-luhr*
special spécial(e) *spess-yal*
speciality la spécialité *spess-yal-eetai*
speed la vitesse *veetess;* **at full speed** à toute vitesse *a toot veetess*
to spell épeler *aiplai*
to spend (money) dépenser *daiponsai,* **or (time)** passer *passai*
spice l'épice [f] *aipeess*
spicy épicé(e) *aipeessai*
spider l'araignée [f] *arainn-yai*
spinach les épinards [m] *aipee-nar*
to spit cracher *krashai*
to split (divide) partager *partajai,* **or (leave)** filer* *feelai;* **to split up (relationship)** se séparer *suh saiparai*
to spoil (ruin) gâcher *gashai,* **or (to damage)** abîmer *abeemmai*
spoiled (child) gâté(e) *ga-tai*
spontaneous spontané(e) *sponta-nai*
spoon la cuillère *kwee-yair*
sport le sport *spor;* **sports centre** le centre sportif *sontr sporteef*
sporty (athletic) sportif *sporteef* f: sportive *sporteev*
spot (pimple) le bouton *booton,* **or (place)** l'endroit [m] *ondrwa*
sprain l'entorse [f] *ontorss*
spring (season) le printemps *pranton,* **or (water)** la source *soorss*
spy l'espion(ne) [m/f] *esp-yon f: esp-yonn*
square (in town) la place *plass,* **or (not trendy)** ringard(e)* *rangar f: rangard*
squash (game) le squash *skwash*
stairs l'escalier [m] *eskall-yai*
stamp le timbre *tambr;* **book of stamps** le carnet de timbres *kar-nai duh tambr*
to stand (bear) supporter *sewportai* **e.g. I can't stand...** je ne supporte pas... **, or (not sit)** être debout *etr duhboo;* **to stand up** se lever *suh luhvai;* **to stand up for** défendre *daifondr*
stand-by (ticket, passenger) le stand-by
star (in sky) l'étoile [f] *aitwal,* **or (of film)** la vedette *vuhdett,* **or** la star
start le début *daibew,* **or (of race)** le départ *daipar*

starter (first course) le hors-d'oeuvre [m] *or duhvr,* **or** l'entrée [f] *ontrai*
station (train) la gare *gar,* **or (underground, radio)** la station *stass-yon* **(see also bus)**
statue la statue *sta-tew*
to stay rester *restai*
steak le steak, **or** l'entrecôte [f] *ontr-kote*
to steal voler *volai*
steep raide *red*
step (footstep) le pas *pa,* **or (stair)** la marche *marsh;* **stepbrother** le demi-frère *duh-mee frair;* **stepfather** le beau-père *bo pair;* **stepmother** la belle-mère *bel mair;* **stepsister** la demi-soeur *duh-mee suhr*
stereo: personal stereo le baladeur *baladuhr*
stereotype le stéréotype *stairai-oteep*
to stick (glue) coller *kolai*
stiff raide *red;* **to be/feel stiff** avoir des courbatures *avwar dai koorbatewr*
still (even now) toujours *toojoor,* **or (not moving)** immobile *ee-mobeel*
to sting piquer *peekai*
stingy (not generous) radin(e) *radan f: radeenn*
to stink puer *pewai*
to stir remuer *ruhmewai,* **or (cause trouble)** provoquer *provokai*
stomach l'estomac [m] *esto-ma,* **or (tummy)** le ventre *vontr;* **upset stomach** l'indigestion [f] *andeejest-yon* **(see also 'ache' picture)**
stone la pierre *pee-air*
to stop arrêter *araitai,* **or (to prevent)** empêcher *ompeshai*
stopover (on journey) l'escale [f] *esskal,* **or** l'étape [f] *aitap*
storm la tempête *tompet,* **or (with thunder)** l'orage [m] *oraj*
story l'histoire [f] *eestwar,* **or (plot)** le scénario *sai-naree-o,* **or (in newspaper)** l'article [m] *arteekl*
straight (not curved) droit(e) *drwa f: drwat,* **or (directly)** directement *deerekt-mon,* **or (old-fashioned)** pas cool* *pa kool,* **or** coincé(e)* *kwansai,* **or (not gay)** hétérosexuel(le) *aitairo-seksewel,* **or** hétéro***;**
straight ahead tout droit *too drwa*
strange étrange *aitronj*
strawberry la fraise *fraiz*
street la rue *rew;* **high/main street** la rue principale *rew pransseepal*
stress le stress
strict strict(e) *streekt*
strike la grève *graiv*
string la ficelle *feessel*
striped rayé(e) *rai-yai*
strong fort(e) *for f: fort*

to ski skier

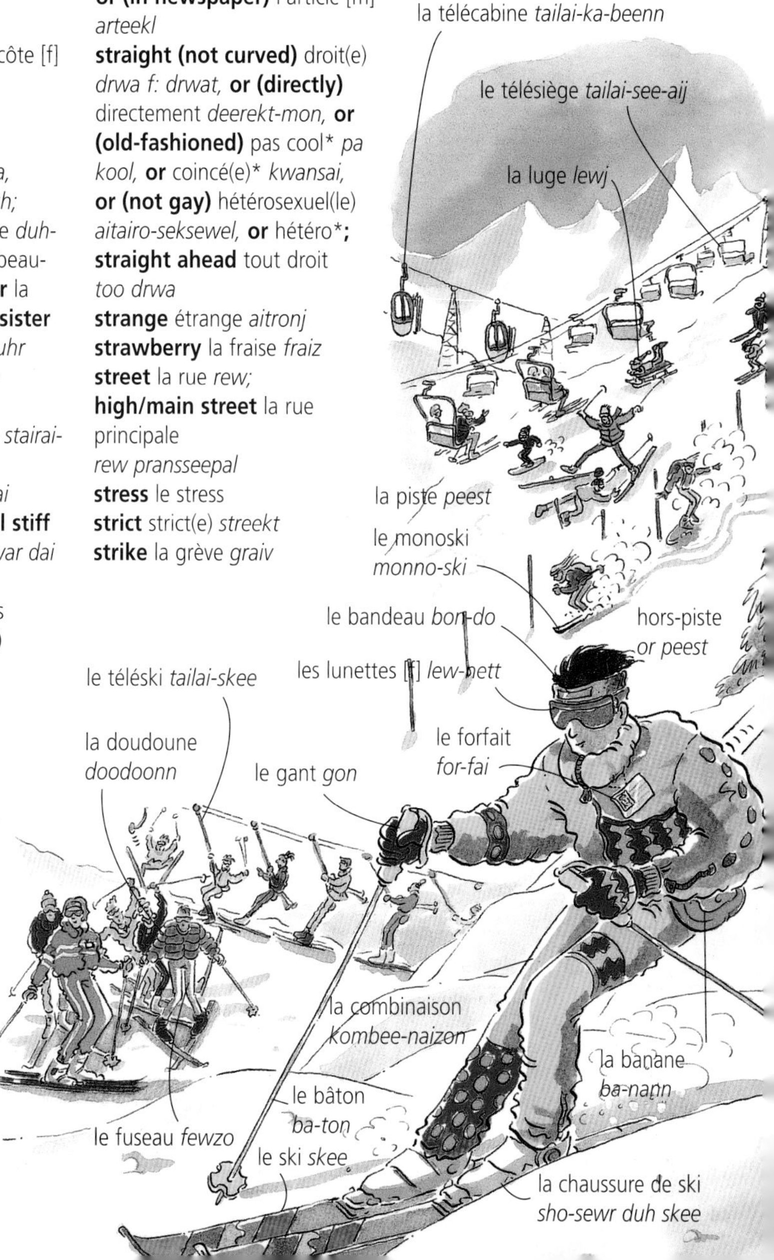

la télécabine *tailai-ka-beenn*
le télésiège *tailai-see-aij*
la luge *lewj*
la piste *peest*
le monoski *monno-ski*
le bandeau *bon-do*
hors-piste *or peest*
les lunettes [f] *lew-nett*
le téléski *tailai-skee*
la doudoune *doodoonn*
le forfait *for-fai*
le gant *gon*
la combinaison *kombee-naizon*
la banane *ba-nann*
le bâton *ba-ton*
le fuseau *fewzo*
le ski *skee*
la chaussure de ski *sho-sewr duh skee*

stubborn têtu(e) *taitew*
stuck (unable to move) coincé(e) *kwansai;* **stuck-up** prétentieux *praitonss-yuh* f: prétentieuse *praitonss-yuhz*
student l'étudiant(e) [m/f] *aitewd-yon f: aitewd-yont*
to study étudier *aitewd-yai*
stuff (things) les trucs* [m] *trewk,* **or** le barda** *barda*
stuffy (no air) mal aéré(e) *mal a-airai*
stunning (amazing) stupéfiant(e) *stewpaif-yon f: stewpaif-yont,* **or (lovely)** extraordinaire *ekstra-ordee-nair;* **she's stunning** elle est canon* *el ai kannon*
stupid stupide *stewpeed,* **or** bête *bet;* **to act stupid** faire l'idiot(e) *fair leed-yo f: ...leed-yot;* **a stupid thing** une bêtise *baiteez*
style le style *steel*
subconsciously inconsciemment *ankonsee-ammon*
subject le sujet *sewjai*
subtitle le sous-titre *soo-teetr*
subtle subtil(e) *sewb-teel*
suburbs la banlieue *bonl-yuh*
to succeed réussir *rai-ewseer*
success le succès *sewksai*
such tellement *tell-mon,* **or** si *see*
suddenly tout à coup *too ta koo*
suede le daim *dam*
to suffer souffrir *soofreer*
sugar le sucre *sewkr*
to suggest proposer *propozai*
suit (man's) le costume *kostewm,* **or (woman's)** le tailleur *tie-yuhr*
to suit (look good) aller bien *allai bee-an;* **it suits you** ça te/vous va bien *sa tuh/voo va bee-an*
suitcase la valise *va-leez*
summer l'été [m] *aitai;* **summer camp** le camp de vacances *kom duh vakonss*
sun le soleil *solaiy;* **sun block** l'écran total [m] *aikron to-tal;* **sun cream** la crème solaire *kremm solair*
to sunbathe se faire bronzer *suh fair bronzai* (see also picture below)
sunburned: to be/get sunburned prendre un coup de soleil *prondr un koo duh solaiy*
Sunday dimanche [m] *dee-monsh*
sunglasses les lunettes de soleil [f] *lew-nett duh solaiy*
sunny ensoleillé(e) *onssolai-yai*
sunset le coucher du soleil *kooshai dew solaiy*
sunstroke l'insolation [f] *anssolass-yon*
superficial superficiel(le) *sewpairfeess-yel*
supermarket le supermarché *sewpair-marshai*
superstitious superstitieux *sewpair-steess-yuh* f: superstitieuse *sewpair-steess-yuhz*
supper le dîner *dee-nai*
supplement le supplément *sewplai-mon*
to suppose supposer *sewpozai*
supposed to censé(e) *sonssai*
sure sûr(e) *sewr*

to sunbathe se faire bronzer

to surf surfer

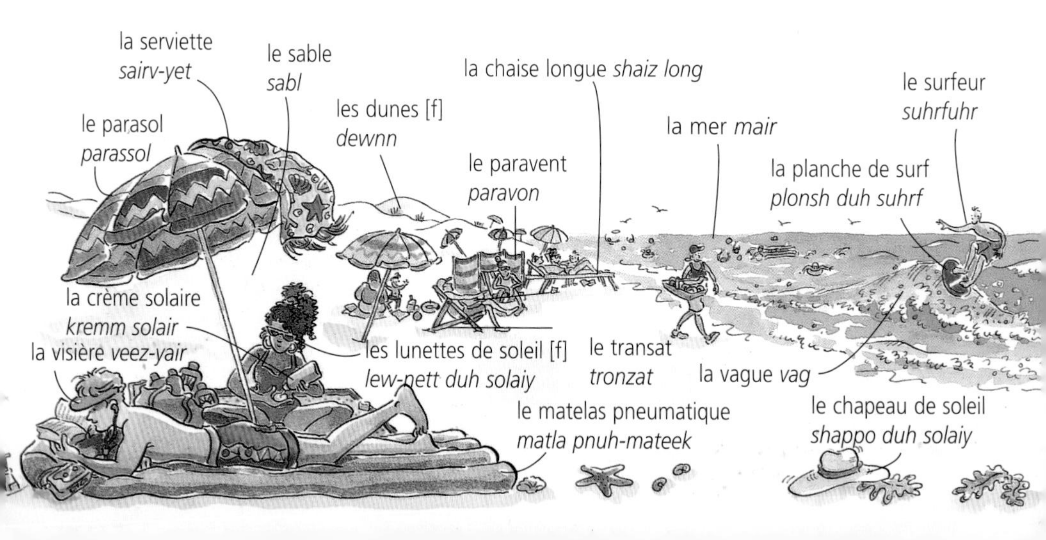

to surf (sport/Internet) surfer *suhrfai* (see also picture below)
surprise la surprise *sewrpreez*
suspense le suspense *sewsponss*
to swallow avaler *avalai*
to swap échanger *aishonjai*
to swear (promise) jurer *jewrai*
swearword le gros mot *gro mo*
sweat la sueur *sewuhr*
to sweat transpirer *tronspeerai*
sweater le pull-over *pewlovair,* **or** le pull
sweatshirt le sweat-shirt
sweet le bonbon *bonbon,* **or (sugary)** sucré(e) *sewkrai,* **or (cute)** mignon(ne) *meenn-yon f: meenn-yonn*
to swim nager *najai,* **or (to go swimming, to go for a dip)** se baigner *suh benn-yai* (see also picture below)
swimming la natation *natass-yon;* **swimming pool** la piscine *peesseenn;* **swimming costume/trunks** le maillot de bain *my-o duh ban*
swing la balançoire *balonswar*
Switzerland la Suisse *sweess*
swollen enflé(e) *enflai*
synagogue la synagogue *see-nagog*

table la table *tabl;* **table football** le baby-foot *baibee foot;* **table tennis** le tennis de table *tai-neess duh tabl*
tacky (unstylish) moche *mosh*
to take prendre *prondr* (see Verbs p.45), **or (to lead)** emmener *omm-nai;* **to take away** emporter *omportai;* **to take off** enlever *onluhvai,* **or (plane)** décoller *daikolai;* **to take part** participer *parteesseepai*
take-away (food) (les plats) à emporter [m] *(pla) a omportai,* **or (café)** l'endroit vente à emporter [m] *ondrwa vont a omportai*
to talk parler *parlai*
talkative bavard(e) *bavar f: bavard*
tall grand(e) *gron f: grond*
tampon le tampon *tompon*
tan le bronzage *bronzaj*
tanned bronzé(e) *bronzai*
tap le robinet *robee-nai*
tapestry la tapisserie *tapeesairee*
tart la tarte *tart,* **or (small)** la tartelette *tartuh-lett*
taste le goût *goo*
to taste (as in "taste it") goûter *gootai,* **or (as in "it tastes sweet")** avoir un goût *avwar un goo*
taxi le taxi *taksee;* **taxi stand** la station de taxis *stass-yon duh taksee*
tea (drink) le thé *tai,* **or (afternoon snack)** le goûter *gootai,* **or (evening meal)** le dîner *dee-nai*
to teach (in school/ university) enseigner *onssainn-yai,* **or (as in "that'll teach him")** apprendre *approndr*
teacher le professeur *professuhr*
team l'équipe [f] *aikeep;* **to be part of a team** faire partie d'une équipe *fair partee dewnn aikeep*
tear: in tears en larmes; **to burst into tears** fondre en larmes *fondr on larm*
to tease taquiner *ta-kee-nai,* **or (to be joking)** plaisanter *plaizontai*
teenager l'adolescent(e) [m/f] *adolesson f: adolessont,* **or** l'ado*
telephone (see phone)
television la télévision *tailaiveez-yon,* **or** la télé*; **on television** à la télé*; **cable TV** le câble *kabl;* **to have cable TV** être câblé(e) *etr kablai;* **digital TV** la télé* numérique *tailai newmaireek*

to swim nager

to tell (say) dire *deer,* **or (recount)** raconter *rakontai;* **to tell off** gronder *grondai,* **or** engueuler** *onguhlai*
temperature la température *tompairatewr;* **to have a temperature** avoir de la fièvre *avwar duh lafee-aivr*
temporary temporaire *tomporair*

what time is it? quelle heure est-il?

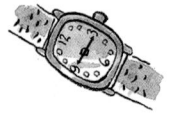

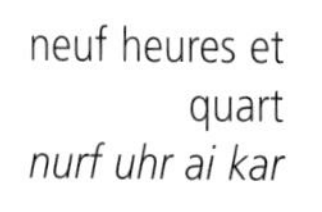
neuf heures et quart *nurf uhr ai kar*

trois heures *trwa-zuhr*

huit heures moins dix *wee-tuhr mwan deess*

onze heures vingt *onz-uhr van*

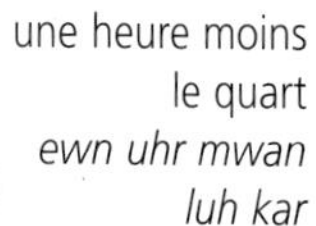
une heure moins le quart *ewn uhr mwan luh kar*

dix heures et demi *deez uhr ai duh-mee*

midi/minuit *meedee/meenn-wee*

tennis le tennis *tai-neess*
tent la tente *tont* (see also campsite)
term (school, university) le trimestre *tree-mestr;* **beginning of term** la rentrée *rontrai*
terrible terrible *tai-reebl*
terrific formidable *for-meedabl,* **or** super *sewpair*
terrorism le terrorisme *terroreesm*
test (at school) l'interrogation [f] *antair-ogass-yon*
textbook le manuel *manewel*
Thames (river) la Tamise *tameez*
than que *kuh,* **or (with numbers)** de *duh*
to thank remercier *ruh-mairss-yai*
thankful (for) reconnaissant(e) de *ruhkonnaisson duh f: ruhkonaissont duh*
thank you merci *mairsee*
that ce† *suh* f: cette *set;* **that one** celui-là *suhlwee-la* f: celle-là *sell-la*
thaw (ice) fondre *fondr,* **or (food)** décongeler *dai-konjuhlai*
the le *luh* f: la *la,* **or (in front of a vowel, or sometimes "h")** l' pl: les *lai* **(see also Nouns p.44)**
theatre le théâtre *tai-atr*
their leur *luhr*
them (as in "I see/know them") les *lai,* **or (as in "it's them" and after "of", "than", "to", "with", etc.)** eux *uh* f: elles *el*
theme le thème *tem;* **theme park** le parc (d'attraction) à thème *park (datraksyon) a tem*
then alors *alor*
therapy la thérapie *tairapee*

there là *la;* **there is/are** il y a *eel-ee-a*
these ces *sai;* **these ones** ceux-ci *suh-see* f: celles-ci *sel-see*
they ils *eel* f: elles *el*
thick épais(se) *aipai f: aipaiss,* **or (stupid)** bête *bet,* **or** lourd(e)* *loor f: loord*
thief le voleur *voluhr* f: la voleuse *voluhz*
thin mince *manss*
thing la chose *shoze,* **or** le truc* *trewk,* **or** le machin* *mash-an*
things (belongings) les affaires [f] *afair*
to think penser *ponsai*
thirsty: to be thirsty avoir soif *avwar swaf*
this ce† *suh* f: cette *set;* **this one** celui-ci *suh-lwee-see* f: celle-ci *sel-see*
those ces *sai;* **those ones** ceux-là *suh-la* f: celles-là *sel-la*
threat la menace *muh-nass*
thrill le frisson *freesson*
thriller le film à suspense *feelm a sewsponss,* **or** le thriller* *treeluhr*
throat la gorge *gorj;* **sore throat** l'angine [f] *onjeenn*
through à travers *a travair;* **to go through** traverser *travairsai*
to throw lancer *lonsai;* **to throw away/out** jeter *juhtai;* **to throw up (be sick)** vomir *vo-meer*
thug le voyou *vwa-yoo*
Thursday jeudi [m] *juhdee*
ticket le billet *bee-yai,* **or** le ticket *teekai;* **ticket machine** le distributeur de billets *dee-stree-bew-tuhr duhbee-yai;* **ticket office** le guichet *geeshai;* **ticket collector** le contrôleur

† ***ce*** changes to ***cet*** (*set*) in front of a [m] word beginning with a vowel or sometimes an "h", e.g. ***cet homme***.

kontroluhr f: la contrôleuse *kontroluhz;* **ticket stamping machine** le composteur *kompostuhr*
to tickle chatouiller *shatoo-yai*
tide la marée *marai*
to tidy up ranger *ronjai*
to tie attacher *atashai,* **or (knot)** nouer *noo-ai*
tights les collants [m] *kolon*
time (hour) l'heure [f] *uhr,* **or (occasion)** la fois *fwa;* **on time** à l'heure**; to have time** avoir le temps *avwar luh ton;* **what time is it?** quelle heure est-il? *kel uhr ai-teel* **(see also picture on opposite page)**
timetable (train/bus) l'horaire [m] *orair,* **or (school)** l'emploi du temps [m] *omplwa dew ton*
tint (for hair) le shampooing colorant *shompwan koloron*
tinted (hair) teint(e) *tan f: tant,* **or (glass)** teinté(e) *tantai*
tiny minuscule *meenew-skewl*
tip (end) le bout *boo,* **or (money)** le pourboire *poorbwar*
tissue (hanky) le mouchoir (en papier) *mooshwar (on pap-yai)*
to à *a* (see also p.45)**, or (with [f] country names)** en *on*
toast le pain grillé *pan gree-yai,* **or** le toast *tost*
today aujourd'hui *o-joor-dwee*
together ensemble *onsombl*
toilet les toilettes [f] *twalett,* **or** les WC [m] *vai sai;* **women's/ men's** dames/messieurs *damm/mess-yuh;* **toilet paper** le papier hygiénique *pap-yai eejaineek*
toll le péage *pai-aj*
tomato la tomate *to-mat;* **tomato sauce** la sauce tomate *sosse to-mat*
tomorrow demain *duh-man*
the day after tomorrow après-demain *aprai-duh-man*
tongue la langue *long*
tonight ce soir *suh swar*
too (too much) trop *tro,* **or (also)** aussi *o-see*
tool l'outil [m] *ootee* **(see also picture below)**
tooth la dent *don* **(see also 'ache' picture)**
tour le voyage organisé *vwa-yaj organneezai*
tourist le/la touriste *tooreest;* **tourist office** l'office du tourisme [m] *ofeess dew tooreesm*
touristy touristique *tooreesteek*
towel la serviette *sairv-yet*
town la ville *veel;* **town centre** le centre-ville *sontr-veel;* **old town** la vieille ville *vee-aiy veel;* **town hall** l'hôtel de ville [m] *otel duh veel*

tools les outils

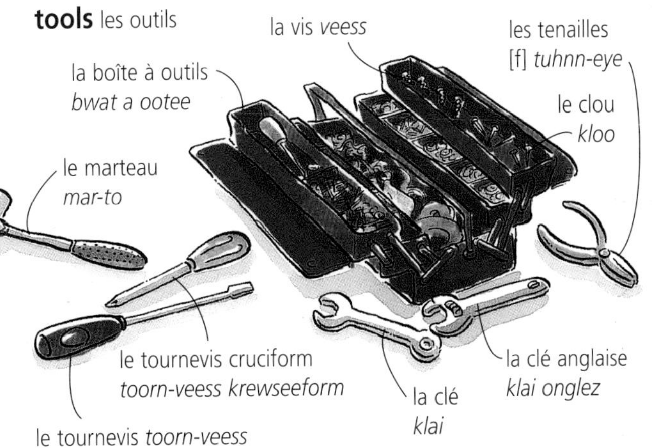

toothbrush la brosse à dents *bross a don*
toothpaste le dentifrice *donteefreess*
top (bottle) le bouchon *booshon,* **or (not bottom, item of clothing)** le haut *o*
torch (pocket) la lampe de poche *lomp duh posh,* **or (flaming)** la torche *torsh*
to touch toucher *tooshai;* **to touch wood** toucher du bois *tooshai dew bwa*
tour (day trip) l'excursion [f] *ekskewrss-yon,* **or (concerts)** la tournée *toor-nai;* **package**
toy le jouet *jooai*
traffic la circulation *seerkewlass-yon;* **traffic jam** l'embouteillage [m] *ombootai-yaj;* **traffic lights** les feux [m] *fuh,* **or** le feu rouge *fuh rooj*
train le train *tran* **(see also picture on p.40)**
to train (for sport) s'entraîner *sontrainnai,* **or (for a job)** former *for-mai*
trainers les baskets [f] *baskett*
tramp le clochard *kloshar,* **or** le clodo** *klodo*
to translate traduire *tradweer*

train le train

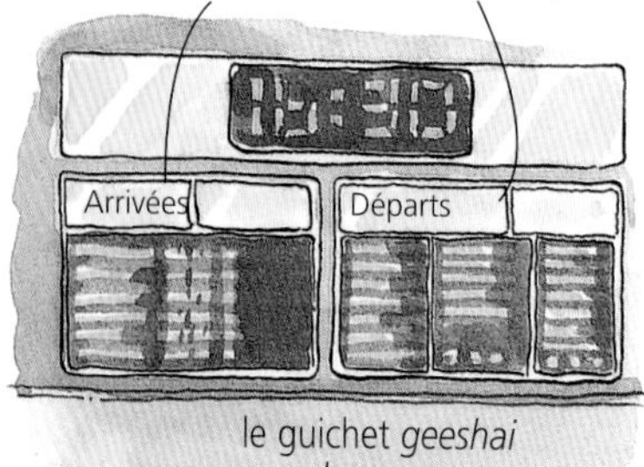

to travel voyager *vwa-yajai*
travel agency *l'agence de voyages* [f] *ajonss duh vwa-yaj*
traveller le voyageur *vwa-yajuhr* f: la voyageuse *vwa-yajuhz;* **traveller's cheque** le traveller's chèque *trav-luhrz shek*
tree l'arbre [m] *arbr*
trendy branché(e)** *bronshai*
trip (long) le voyage *vwa-yaj,* **or (short)** l'excursion [f] *ekskewrss-yon*
trolley (for baggage/shopping) le chariot *sharee-o*
trouble les ennuis [m] *onnwee*
trousers le pantalon *pontalon*
true vrai(e) *vrai*
to trust avoir confiance *avwar konf-yonss*
truth la vérité *vaireetai*
to try essayer *essai-yai*
T-shirt le tee-shirt
Tuesday mardi [m] *mardee*
tuna le thon *ton*
tunnel le tunnel *tewnell*
to turn tourner *toor-nai;* **to turn around/back** faire demi-tour *fair duh-mee toor;* **to turn down (music/heat)** baisser *baissai;* **to turn off (light/TV)** éteindre *aitandr;* **to turn on (light/TV)** allumer *alew-mai;* **to turn up (music/heat)** monter *montai,* **or (arrive)** arriver *areevai*
twin (brother/sister) le jumeau *jew-mo* f: la jumelle *jew-mell*
typical typique *teepeek*
tyre le pneu *pnuh;* **tyre pressure** la pression (de gonflage) *press-yon (duh gonflaj)*

ugly laid(e) *lai f: laid*
umbrella le parapluie *paraplwee*
unbelievable incroyable *ankrwayabl*
under sous *soo*
underground (trains) le métro *maitro*
to understand comprendre *komprondr*
underwear les sous-vêtements [m] *soo-vet-mon*
unemployed (person) le chômeur *shommuhr* f: la chômeuse *shommuhz,* **or (out of work)** au chômage *o shommaj*
unemployment le chômage *shommaj*
unfortunately malheureusement *maluh-ruhz-mon*
United States les États-Unis [m] *aita-zewnnee*
university l'université [f] *ewnnee-vairsee-tai*
unusual (rare) rare *rar,* **or (different)** original(e) *oreejeennal*
up: to go/walk up monter *montai*
uptight coincé(e)** *kwansai*
urgent urgent(e) *ewrjon f: ewrjont*
us nous *noo*
to use se servir de *suh sairveer duh*
used: to be used to avoir l'habitude de *avwar labeetewd duh*
useful utile *ewteel*
useless (of no use) inutile *eennewteel,* **or (no good)** nul(le)* *newl*
usual (customary) habituel(le) *abeetew-el;* **as usual** comme d'habitude *komm dabeetewd*
usually d'habitude *dabeetewd*

vacation les vacances [f] *vakonss*
vaccination la vaccination *vakseennass-yon*
valid valable *valabl*
valuables les objets de valeur [m] *objai duh valuhr*

value la valeur *valuhr*
vanilla la vanille *vanneey*
vegan végétalien(ne) *vaijaital-yan f: vaijaital-yenn*
vegetable le légume *laigewmm*
vegetarian végétarien(ne) *vaijaitar-yan f: vaijaitar-yenn*
vending machine le distributeur automatique *dee-stree-bew-tuhr otommateek*
very très *trai,* **or** vachement* *vash-mon;* **very much** beaucoup *bo-koo*
view la vue *vew,* **or (opinion)** l'avis [m] *avee*
village le village *veelaj*
vine la vigne *veenn-yuh*
vineyard le vignoble *veenn-yobl*
visit la visite *veezeet*
to visit (a place) visiter *veezeetai,* **or (a person)** rendre visite à *rondr veezeet a*
vital indispensable *andeess-ponsabl*
volleyball le volley(-ball) *volai(-bal)*
vote le vote *vote*

wacky farfelu(e) *farfuh-lew,* **or** dingue* *dang,* **or** original(e) *oreejeennal*
to waffle parler pour ne rien dire *parlai poor nuh ree-an deer,* **or** radoter* *ra-dotai*
wage la paye *paiy*
waist la taille *tie-y*
waistcoat le gilet *jeelai*
to wait attendre *a-tondr*
waiter le serveur *sairvuhr*
waiting room la salle d'attente *sal da-tont*
waitress la serveuse *sairvuhz*
to wake up se réveiller *suh raivai-yai*
Wales le pays de Galles *pai-ee duh gal*
wall le mur *mewr*
walk la promenade *promm-nad,* **or** la balade* *balad,* **or** la randonnée *rondonnai*
to walk marcher *marshai,* **or (to go on foot)** aller à pied *allai a pee-ai;* **to walk around/about** se promener *suh promm-nai*
wallet le portefeuille *portuh-fuh-y*
to want vouloir *voolwar* **(see Verbs p.45)**
war la guerre *gair*
wardrobe l'armoire [f] *armwar*
warm (assez) chaud(e) *(assai) sho f: ...shode*
to warm up réchauffer *raishofai,* **or (for a sport)** s'échauffer *saishofai*
warning l'avertissement [m] *avairteess-mon*
wart la verrue *verew*
to wash laver *lavai,* **or (yourself)** se laver**;** **to wash up** faire la vaisselle *fair la vaissell* **washing:** **washing machine** le lave-linge *lav-lanj;* **washing powder** la lessive *laisseev;* **washing-up** la vaisselle *vaissell;* **washing-up liquid** le liquide vaisselle *leekeed vaissell*
wasp la guêpe *gaip*
waste (of food/money etc.) le gaspillage *gaspee-yaj;* **waste of time** la perte de temps *pairt duh ton*

water l'eau

l'eau minérale plate [f] *o mee-nairal platt*
la cascade *kaskad*
le glaçon *glasson*
l'eau minérale gazeuse [f] *o mee-nairal*
la carafe *karaf*
un verre d'eau *un vair doh*

wine le vin

le rouge *rooj*
le blanc *blon*
le rosé *rozai*
la demi-bouteille *duh-mee bootaiy*
le pichet *peeshai*
le tire-bouchon *teer booshon*
le bouchon *booshon*
un verre de vin *un vair duh van*

to waste (food/money) gaspiller *gaspee-yai,* **or (time/opportunity)** perdre *pairdr*
watch la montre *montr*
to watch (look at) regarder *ruhgardai,* **or (keep an eye on)** surveiller *sewrvai-yai;* **watch out!** attention! *attonss-yon,* **or (to a friend)** fais gaffe!* *fai gaf*
water l'eau [f] *o*
(see also picture on p 41)
waterproof imperméable *ampair-mai-abl*
way (direction) la direction *deereks-yon,* **or (route)** le chemin *shuh-man,* **or (manner)** la façon *fasson;* **to be/get in the way** gêner *jennai;* **to get your own way** arriver à ses fins *areevai a sai fan;* **no way!** pas question! *pa kest-yon*
we nous *noo,* **or** on *on*
weak faible *faibl,* **or (coffee, tea)** léger *laijai* f: légère *laijair*
to wear porter *portai;* **to wear out (exhaust)** épuiser *aipweezai,* **or (overuse)** user *ewzai*
wealthy riche *reesh;*
weather le temps *ton;* **what's the weather like?** quel temps fait-il? *kel ton fai-teel;* **weather forecast** la météo *maitai-o*
(see also picture below)
website le site web *seet web*
Wednesday mercredi [m] *mairkruh-dee*
week la semaine *suh-menn*
weekend le week-end
weight le poids *pwa;* **to lose weight** maigrir *maigreer;* **to put on weight** grossir *grosseer*
weird bizarre *beezar*
welcome bienvenu(e) *bee-an-vuh-new;* **you're welcome!** de rien! *duh ree-an*
well bien *bee-an;* **well-behaved** sage *saj;* **well-cooked** bien cuit(e) *bee-an kwee f: ...kweet;* **well-known** très connu(e) *trai konnew;* **to be well** aller bien *allai bee-an*
Welsh gallois(e) *galwa f: galwaz*
west l'ouest [m] *oo-est*
wet mouillé(e) *moo-yai*
what (as in "what?") quoi *kwa,* **or (as in "what do you want?")** qu'est-ce que *kess-kuh;* **what is this/it?** qu'est-ce que c'est? *kess-kuh sai;* **about/in/with what?** de/dans/avec quoi? *duh/don/avek kwa;* **what a...! (as in "what a great hat!")** quel(le)...! *kel*
wheel la roue *roo;* **steering wheel** le volant *volon*
wheelchair le fauteuil roulant *fotuh-y roolon*
when quand *kon*
where où *oo*
which (as in "which [one]?") lequel *luhkel* f: laquelle *lakell,* **or (as in "which bike/cake etc?")** quel(le) *kel*
while (during) pendant que *pondon kuh*
to whistle siffler *seeflai*
white blanc *blon* f: blanche *blonsh*
who qui *kee;* **whose** à qui *a kee*
whole entier *ont-yai* f: entière *ont-yair*
why pourquoi *poorkwa*
wide large *larj*
widow la veuve *verv*
widower le veuf *verf*

weather
le temps

il pleut *eel pluh*

c'est couvert *sai koovair*

il fait beau *eel fai bo*

il neige *eel naij*

wild (not tame) sauvage *sovaj;* **to be/go wild (about)** être/devenir fou (de) *etr/duh-vuh-neer foo (duh)* f: ...folle *...fol*

to win gagner *gann-yai*

wind le vent *von* **(see also picture below)**

windmill le moulin à vent *moolan a von*

window la fenêtre *fuh-netr,* **or (shop)** la vitrine *veetreenn*

windscreen le pare-brise *par-breez;* **windscreen wiper** l'essuie-glace [m] *esswee-gla-ss*

windsurfer (board) la planche à voile *plonsh a vwal,* **or (person)** le/la planchiste *plonsheest*

wine le vin *van* **(see also picture on p.41);**

wine-tasting la dégustation *daigewstass-yon*

winner le/la gagnant(e) *gann-yon f: gann-yont*

winter l'hiver [m] *eevair*

wish le voeu *vuh;* **best wishes (in a letter)** amitiés *ammeet-yai,* **or (Christmas, birthday)** meilleurs voeux *mai-yuhr vuh*

to wish (hope) souhaiter *soo-aitai*

with avec *avek*

without sans *son*

woman la femme *famm,* **or (lady)** la dame *damm*

wonderful formidable *for-meedabl*

wood le bois *bwa*

wool la laine *lenn*

word le mot *mo;* **words (of song)** les paroles [f] *parol*

work le travail *trav-eye,* **or** le boulot** *boolo*

to work travailler *trav-eye-ai,* **or** bosser** *bossai,* **or (function)** marcher *marshai*

world le monde *mond;* **out of this world** extraordinaire *ekstra-ordee-nair*, **or** extra*

worried inquiet *ank-yai* f: inquiète *ank-yet*

to worry s'inquiéter *sank-yaitai*

worse pire *peer*

worth: to be worth valoir *valwar*

wound la blessure *blessewr*

wrinkle la ride *reed*

wrist le poignet *pwanyai*

to write écrire *aikreer*

writer l'écrivain [m] *aikreevan*

wrong (incorrect) faux *fo* f: fausse *fosse,* **or (unfair)** injuste *anjewst;* **to be wrong (not right)** avoir tort *avwar tor,* **or (mistaken)** se tromper *suh trompai;* **what's wrong?** qu'est-ce qui ne va pas? *kess kee nuh va pa*

to yawn bâiller *buy-ai*

year l'année [f] *annai*

yellow jaune *jone*

yes oui *wee,* **or (after negative question)** si *see*

yesterday hier *ee-yair*

yogurt le yaourt *ya-oort*

you (as in "you like him") tu *tew,* **or** vous *voo,* **or (as in "it's you" and after "and", "for", "than", etc.)** toi *twa,* **or** vous *voo,* **or (as in "he knows you")** te *tuh,* **or** vous *voo*

young jeune *juhnn*

your (to friend) ton *ton* f: ta *ta* pl: tes *tai,* **or (polite form)** votre *votr* pl: vos *vo*

youth hostel l'auberge de jeunesse [f] *o-bairj duh juhnness*

zero zéro *zairo*

zip la fermeture éclair *fair-muh-tewr*

il y a un orage *eel ee a unnoraj*

il fait froid *eel fai frwa*

il fait chaud *eel fai sho*

il fait du vent *eel fai dew von*

You don't have to make a perfect sentence to be understood, but knowing a little about the way French works will help. These notes provide some basic tips about the language.

Nouns *(names of things, e.g. "guitar")*

Most French nouns are either masculine or feminine. The words for "the" (**le** or **la**) and "a" (**un** or **une**) can tell you which each is. **Le** and **un** are used with masculine nouns, **la** and **une** with feminine ones. With nouns that begin with a vowel (and sometimes "h") though, "the" is **l'**.

In English you often drop "the", but this is unusual in French, e.g. **j'aime le chocolat** = I like chocolate.

Adjectives *(describing words, e.g. "red")*

Unlike English adjectives, many French ones have two forms - one to use with masculine nouns and one with feminine nouns, e.g. **le pull vert** = the green sweater, **la jupe verte** = the green skirt.

Another difference is that they come after the word they describe, e.g. **le teeshirt bleu** = the blue T-shirt. However, a few common ones come before:

beau/belle (beautiful)
gentil/(le) (nice, kind)
gros(se) (large, fat)
grand(e) (big, tall)
mauvais(e) (bad)
vieux/vieille (old)
joli(e) (pretty)
bon(ne) (good)
jeune (young)
long(ue) (long)
petit(e) (small)

Plurals *(more than one, e.g. "guitars")*

The plural word for "the" is **les**. Most nouns and adjectives are made plural by adding an "s" (or "x" for words that end in **eau, au** or **eu**), e.g. **les pulls verts** = the green sweaters. Words ending in **al** change to **aux**, e.g. **l'animal/les animaux** = animal/animals

The plural "s" or "x" are not pronounced unless the next word begins with a vowel (or often "h"). Then the "s" or "x" sounds like a "z", e.g. **les îles** laiz-eel = the islands.

Using tu and vous

French has two words for "you": **tu** and **vous** (and for related words, e.g. **ton** and **votre** both mean "your"). You use the casual **tu** for a friend, relative or someone your own age or younger. Use the polite **vous** for an adult you don't know well. For more than one person, always use **vous**. If in doubt, use **vous** (and related words, e.g. **votre**).

Verbs *(action words, e.g. "to speak")*

Most French verbs end in "er" in the infinitive (the basic form, e.g. **parler** = to speak) and follow the same pattern for each tense (present, future, past, etc.).

For the present tense, drop **er** and add the endings underlined below:

I speak[1] **je parle**
you speak **tu parles**
he/she/it speaks **il/elle parle**
we speak **nous parlons**
you speak **vous parlez**
they speak **ils/elles parlent**

To say things about the past, use the present of **avoir** = to have, or for a few verbs **être** = to be (see box below) with something called the past participle. You make this by replacing **er** with **é**, e.g. **j'ai parlé** = I spoke/have spoken.

To talk about the future; use the present tense of **aller** (to go) with the infinitive, e.g. **je vais parler** = I am going to speak.

Some verbs don't follow these guidelines. Below are the present and past tenses of some particularly useful ones:

	aller (to go)	**avoir** (to have)
present:	**je vais**	**j'ai**
	tu vas	**tu as**
	il/elle va	**il/elle a**
	nous allons	**nous avons**
	vous allez	**nous avez**
	ils/elles vont	**ils/elles ont**
past:	**être + allé(e)**	**avoir + eu**

1: All French present tense verbs can be translated by the "am/are/is ...ing" version in English, e.g. **je parle** can mean "I speak" or "I am speaking".

Reflexive verbs *(verbs with "se")*

Some French verbs, called reflexive verbs, begin with **se** in the infinitive (**s'** before a vowel or "h"). They usually mean an action you do to yourself, e.g. **se raser** = to shave. With **je** use **me**, with **tu** use te, with **il(s)** and **elle(s)** use **se**, with **nous** use **nous** and with **vous** use **vous**, e.g. **je me rase, tu te rases, il se rase, nous nous rasons, etc**.

Questions

French has lots of ways of making a question. The simplest is to raise your voice at the end of a sentence. **Je dois partir** = I have to go, becomes: **Je dois partir?** = Do I have to go?

Another easy way is to start with **est-ce que**, e.g. **Est-ce que je dois partir?** = Do I have to go?

Negatives

To make a verb negative, put **ne** and **pas** (not) on either side, e.g. **je veux** = I want to; **je ne veux pas** = I don't want to

You do the same with other negatives such as **ne... rien** = nothing, and **ne... personne** = nobody.

In everyday French, people often drop the **ne**.

Shortening je, de, ne, etc.

When a two-letter word ending in "e" (**je**, **de**, **ne**, etc.) comes before a word beginning with a vowel (or "h") you usually replace the "e" by an apostrophe, e.g. **j'aime** = I like, **je n'aime pas** = I don't like.

Using à and de with le and les

À and de are little words that are used a lot. **À** usually means "to" or "at" and **de** usually means "from" or "of". When followed by **le** or **les** (the), they form one word like this: **à + le = au; à + les = aux; de + le = du; de + les = des**; e.g. **au ciné** = to the cinema.

Possession

The French use **de** (of) to say whose something (or somebody) is, e.g. **le manteau de Sophie** = Sophie's coat; **le père de Patrick** = Patrick's father.

Being polite

A few polite words make all the difference when you approach strangers. Remember **pardon**, **merci** and **s'il vous plaît** (excuse me, thank you and please). Another tip is to add **Monsieur/Madame/ Mademoiselle** (sir/madam/miss) to these expressions and when you greet people, e.g. **Bonjour, Madame** is more polite than just **Bonjour**.

Pronunciation

The best way to pronounce French well is to copy a French speaker. The pronunciation hints in the English-French list (p.4-43) will help. Below are a few extra tips:
- "j" is very soft in French, like the "s" in the English word "pleasure"
- "r" is slightly growled. It is made at the back of the throat;
- "n" and "m" are often barely pronounced after a vowel. Instead they make the vowel sound nasal, as if you were holding your nose. In the pronunciation hints you will see nn or mm when the "n" or "m" is clearly said and Just n or m for the nasal sound.

être (to be)	**faire** (to make/do)	**pouvoir** (can)	**prendre** (to take)	**vouloir** (to want)
je suis **tu es** **il/elle est** **nous sommes** **vous êtes** **ils/elles sont**	**e fais** **tu fais** **il/elle fait** **nous faisons** **vous faites** **ils/elles font**	**je peux** **tu peux** **il/elle peut** **nous pouvons** **vous pouvez** **ils/elles peuvent**	**je prends** **tu prends** **il/elle prend** **nous prenons** **vous prenez** **ils/elles prennent**	**je veux** **tu veux** **il/elle veut** **nous voulons** **vous voulez** **ils/elles veulent**
avoir + été	**avoir + fait**	**avoir + pu**	**avoir + pris**	**avoir + voulu**

à at, or to, or in (see also p.45)
l'abeille [f] bee
abîmer to damage, or to spoil
abonner to take out a subscription
l'abricot [m] apricot
l'accent [m] accent
accepter to accept
l'accident [m] accident
accrocher to hang (up)
l'accueil [m] reception, or welcome
accueillir to welcome
acheter to buy
l'acteur [m] actor
l'actrice [f] actress
l'addition [f] sum, or bill
l'adolescent(e) or **l'ado* [m/f]** teenager
adorer to love, or to adore
l'adresse [f] address
l'adulte [m/f] adult
l'adversaire [m/f] opponent
l'aérobic [m] aerobics
l'aéroglisseur [m] hovercraft
l'aéroport [m] airport
les affaires [f] things, or business; **une bonne affaire** a bargain
l'affiche [f] poster, or notice
affreux (f: affreuse) awful
l'Afrique [f] Africa
agacer to annoy
l'âge [m] age
l'agence de voyages [f] travel agency
l'agenda [m] diary
l'agent (de police) [m] (police) officer
l'agneau [m] lamb
agresser to attack; **se faire agresser** to get mugged
l'aide [f] help, or aid
aider to help
l'aiguille [f] needle
l'ail [m] garlic
ailleurs somewhere else
aimer to like, or to love; **aimer bien** to like
l'air [m] air; **en plein air** in the open air; **air conditionné** air-conditioned
aise: à l'aise comfortable
ajouter to add
l'album [m] album
l'alcool [m] alcohol
alcoolisé(e) alcoholic
l'Algérie [f] Algeria
l'Allemagne [f] Germany
aller (see p.44) to go, or to fit, or to suit; **s'en aller** to leave
l'aller [m] the journey out;
l'aller-retour return (journey/ticket); **l'aller simple** single
l'allergie [f] allergy
s'allonger to lie down
allumer to light, or to switch on
l'allumette [f] match
alors then, or so
l'alpinisme [m] mountaineering
l'amande [f] almond
l'ambassade [f] embassy
l'ambulance [f] ambulance
l'amende [f] fine
amener to bring
amer (f: amère) bitter
américain(e) American
l'Amérique [f] America
l'ami(e) [m/f] friend; **le/la petit(e) ami(e)** boy/girlfriend
l'amitié [f] friendship; **amitiés** best wishes
l'amour [m] love;
les amours [f] love-life;
amoureux (f: amoureuse) in love
l'ampoule [f] lightbulb, or blister
amusant(e) fun, or funny
s'amuser to have fun
l'an [m] year
l'ananas [m] pineapple
l'ancre [f] anchor
l'andouillette [f] spicy sausage made from tripe
l'angine [f] sore throat
anglais(e) English
l'Angleterre [f] England
angoissant(e) nerve-racking
animé(e) lively
l'année [f] year
l'anniversaire [m] birthday, or anniversary
l'annonce [f] advertisement; **les petites annonces** classified ads
l'annuaire [m] phone directory
annuler to cancel
l'antibiotique [m] antibiotic
antiseptique antiseptic
l'antivol [m] lock (for bikes/cars)
août August
l'appareil-photo [m] camera
l'appartement or **l'appart*** [m] flat
l'appel [m] call
appeler to call
s'appeler to be called
l'appétit [m] appetite; **bon appétit** enjoy your meal
apporter to bring
apprendre to learn, or to teach
s'approcher to get/come near
appuyer to press
après after
l'après-midi [m/f] afternoon
arabe Arab
l'araignée [f] spider
l'arbitre [m] umpire
l'arbre [m] tree
l'arc-en-ciel [m] rainbow
l'arête [f] fish bone, or ridge
l'argent [m] money; **l'argent liquide [m]** cash
l'argot [m] slang
l'arnaque: c'est de** l'arnaque** it's a rip-off
l'arrêt [m] stop; **l'arrêt de bus** bus stop; **les arrêts de jeu** injury time
arrêter to arrest, or to stop
les arrhes [f] deposit
l'arrière [m] back (not front)
arriver to arrive, or to happen;
arriver à (faire quelque chose) to manage to (do something)
l'art [m] art
l'article [m] article
l'artisanat [m] crafts
l'artiste [m/f] artist
l'ascenseur [m] lift
l'Asie [f] Asia
l'aspirateur vacuum cleaner
l'aspirine [f] aspirin
s'asseoir to sit down
assez enough, or quite
l'assiette [f] plate; **l'assiette anglaise** plate of cold meats
assis(e) sitting down
l'assurance [f] insurance
l'asthme [m] asthma
l'atelier [m] workshop
attacher to fasten
attendre to wait
l'attention [f] attention, or care;
faire attention to be careful;
attention! watch out!
attraper to catch
l'auberge [f] inn; **l'auberge de jeunesse [f]** youth hostel
augmenter to increase
aujourd'hui today
au revoir goodbye
aussi also, or too; **aussi... que** as... as
l'Australie [f] Australia
australien(ne) Australian
l'auteur [m/f] author

authentique genuine
l'autocollant [m] sticker
automatique automatic
l'automne [m] autumn
l'autoroute [f] motorway
l'auto-stoppeur (f: l'auto-stoppeuse) hitch-hiker
autour around
autre other
l'autre [m/f] the other one
avaler to swallow
avance: en avance early
avancer to go/move forwards
avant before; **avant-hier** the day before yesterday
l'avant [m] front
l'avantage [m] advantage
avec with
aventureux (f: aventureuse) adventurous
avertir to warn
l'avertissement [m] warning
aveugle blind
l'avion [m] plane
l'avis [m] opinion
l'avocat [m] avocado, or (f: l'avocate) lawyer
avoir (see p.44) to have;
se faire avoir* to be had/tricked
avril April

le baby-foot table football
les bagages [m] luggage
la bagarre* fight
la bagnole* car
la bague ring
la baguette French bread
se baigner to go for a swim
bâiller to yawn
le bain bath; **prendre un bain de soleil** to sunbathe
baisser to lower
le bal dance
la balade walk, or outing
le baladeur personal stereo
Balance (star sign) Libra
le balayeur road sweeper
le balcon balcony
balèze** terrific, or strong
la balle ball
les balles** slang for euros
le ballet ballet
le ballon ball, or balloon
la banane banana
le banc bench
la bande band, or bandage, or gang; **la bande dessinée** comic book/strip
le bandeau headband
la banlieue suburbs
la banque bank
le bar bar
baratiner** to chat up, or to natter
la barbe beard
le barda** things, or stuff
la barque boat
la barre bar, or (sailing) tiller
la barrette hair-slide
bas(se) low; **en bas** down below, or downstairs
le basket basketball
les baskets [f] basketball shoes, or trainers
le bateau boat
le bâtiment building
le bâton stick, or pole
la batte bat
la batterie battery, or drums
le batteur drummer
se battre to fight
le baudrier (climbing) harness
bavarder to chat, or to gossip
la bavette (food) type of steak
la BD (la bande dessinée) comic book/strip
beau (f: belle) beautiful, or good-looking; **il fait beau** it's fine weather; **le beau-père** stepfather, or father-in-law
beaucoup many, or a lot
le beauf* short for **le beau-frère** brother-in-law, (but used as derogatory term for a narrow-minded man who lacks taste)
la bécane** motorbike
le beignet doughnut
bêler to bleat
belge Belgian
la Belgique Belgium
Bélier (star sign) Aries
belle (see 'beau');
la belle-mère stepmother, or mother-in-law
bénévole voluntary, or unpaid
le bermuda Bermuda shorts, or long swimming trunks
le besoin need; **avoir besoin de** to need
la bestiole* bug (insect)
bête silly, or stupid
la bêtise stupid thing; **dire des bêtises** to talk nonsense
le beurre butter
la bibliothèque library
le bide** belly; **être/faire un bide**** to be a flop
bien well, or good; **bien cuit(e)** well-cooked; **bien frais** nice and cold; **aller bien** to be well
bientôt soon; **à bientôt** see you soon
bienvenu(e) welcome
la bière beer;
la bière blonde lager;
la bière brune bitter
le bifteck steak
les bijoux [m] jewellery
le billet ticket; **le billet de 10 euros** 10 euro note;
le billet doux love letter
le biscuit biscuit
la bise kiss
le bisou kiss
bizarre odd, or weird
la blague joke
blaguer* to joke
blanc(he) white
la blessure injury
bleu(e) blue
le bleu bruise
blond(e) blond
le/la blond(e) the blond guy/girl
le blouson short, bomber-style jacket
le boeuf beef
boire to drink
le bois wood
la boisson drink
la boîte box, or can, or **(slang)** office, or night-club; **la boîte à outils** tool box; **aller en boîte*** to go clubbing
le bol bowl; **pas de bol!*** no luck! (see also 'ras le bol'*)
la bombe bomb, or riding hat
la bôme (sailing) boom
bon(ne) good
le bonbon sweet
bonjour hello
le bonnet hat; **le bonnet de bain** swimming cap
bonsoir good evening
la bosse bump, or lump, or (skiing) mogle
bosser** to work
la botte boot; **la botte de caoutchouc** welly; **la botte d'équitation** riding boot
la bouche mouth
la boucherie butcher's shop
le bouchon de l'objectif lens cap
bouclé(e) curly
la boucle buckle, or curl;
la boucle d'oreille earring
le boudin black pudding
la bouée buoy, or rubber ring

la bouffe** grub (food)
bouffer** to scoff (eat)
bouger to move
la bougie candle
bouilli(e) boiled
le bouillon broth, or thin soup
le bouillabaisse fish soup
la boulangerie bakery
boules bowling game played with heavy metal balls
le boulot* job, or work; le petit boulot* weekend/holiday job
le bouquin* book
bourré(e)* jam-packed, or (slang) drunk; **bourré(e) de fric**** loaded (with money)
la bourse purse, or grant, or **(la Bourse)** Stock Exchange
bousiller** to wreck
la boussole compass
le bout end, or tip
la bouteille bottle; **la bouteille d'oxygène** oxygen bottle
la boutique shop
le bouton button, or spot
le bowling ten pin bowling
le bracelet bracelet
branché(e)** trendy
brancher to plug in, or (slang) to flirt, or to chat up; **ça (ne) me branche pas**** it doesn't appeal to me
le bras arm
le brassard (de natation) armband (for swimming)
la brasse breast-stroke
la brasserie large restaurant with a bar and café
le bric-à-brac junk
la bride (riding) bridle
la brioche soft, slightly sweet bun or loaf
le briquet lighter
la brocante second-hand furniture/things
le brocanteur junk/second-hand dealer
la broche brooch
la brochette kebab
le bronzage tan
bronzé(e) tanned
se bronzer (or **se faire bronzer**) to sunbathe
la brosse brush; **la brosse à cheveux** hairbrush
le brouillard fog
le bruit noise; **le bruit qui court** rumour
brûler to burn
brun(e) brown
le bureau office, or desk
le bus bus
le but goal

ça this, or that; **ça va** OK, or all right, or (question) how are you?
la cabine cabin; **la cabine téléphonique** phone booth
la cacahuète peanut
cacher to hide
le cadeau present
le cadenas padlock
le cafard cockroach; **avoir le cafard*** to be/feel down
le café café, or (black) coffee; **le café-crème** coffee with cream/milk
cailler** to be freezing cold
la caisse check-out (cash till), or crate (box)
la calculette calculator
le caleçon leggings
calme calm
calmer to calm down
la calorie calorie; **à basses calories** low-calorie
le cambriolage burglary
le caméscope camcorder
le camion lorry
la campagne countryside
camper to camp
le camping campsite; **le camping-car** camper van; **le camping-gaz** camping stove, or camping gas
le Canada Canada
le canal canal
le canap**é sofa, couch**
le canard duck
Cancer (star sign) Cancer
le canif penknife
le canoë canoe
le canon canon; **elle est canon*** she's stunning
le canot small boat
la capitale capital (city)
Capricorne (star sign) Capricorn
le car coach
la carafe jug
la caravane caravan
le carnaval carnival
le carnet notebook
la carotte carrot
le carrefour crossroads
la carrière career
la carte card, or map, or menu; **la carte d'abonnement** season ticket; **la carte bleue** visa card; **la carte de crédit** credit card; **la carte postale** postcard; **la carte routière** road map; **la carte téléphonique** phonecard
le cas case; **au cas où** in case
la cascade waterfall
le casque helmet
la casquette cap
le casse-croûte snack
le casse-noix nutcracker
casser to break; **casse-bonbons*/casse-pieds*** really annoying
se casser to get broken, or (slang) to leave, or to go; **casse-toi!**** get lost!
la casserole saucepan
le cassis blackcurrant
le cassoulet meat and bean casserole
la catastrophe disaster
la cathédrale cathedral
catholique catholic
le cauchemar nightmare
la cause cause; **à cause de** because of
la caution deposit
le cavalier (f: la cavalière) rider, or dance partner
la cave cellar
la caverne cave
le CD CD; **le lecteur de CD** CD player
ce (f: cette) this, or that
céder to give in, or to give way
la ceinture belt; **la ceinture de plomb** weight belt; **la ceinture porte-billets** money belt
célèbre famous
célibataire single (unmarried)
celle (see 'celui')
celui (f: celle) the one; **celui-ci** this one; **celui-là** that one
le cendrier ashtray
censé(e): être censé(e) (faire quelque chose) to be supposed to (do something)
le centime (100 centimes equals one euro)
le centre centre; **le centre commercial** shopping centre; **le centre sportif** sports centre; **le centre-ville** town centre
les céréales [f] cereal
le cerf-volant kite
la cerise cherry
la cervelle brain
ces these, or those

c'est it is
cette (see 'ce')
chacun(e) each one
la chaîne chain, or TV channel; **la chaîne hi-fi** hi-fi system
la chaise chair; **la chaise longue** deck-chair
la chambre room, or bedroom; **la chambre d'hôte** bed and breakfast (guest house)
le champignon mushroom
la chance luck
le change exchange; **le bureau de change** foreign exchange office; **le taux de change** exchange rate
changer to change
la chanson song
chanter to sing
le chanteur (f: la chanteuse) singer
la Chantilly (or **la crème Chantilly**) whipped cream
le chapeau hat; **le chapeau de soleil** sunhat
chaque each
la charcuterie meat products such as ham, salami, pâté, etc. or shop selling these
le chariot trolley (for shopping/ luggage)
le chat cat
le château castle
le chaton kitten
chatouiller to tickle
chaud(e) hot
le chauffage heating
le chauffeur driver
la chaussette sock
le chausson slipper, or pump; **le chausson d'escalade** climbing shoe; **le chausson aux pommes** apple turnover
la chaussure shoe, or (walking/ ski) boot
chauve bald
le chef chef, or boss; **le chef de gare** station master
le chemin path, or route, or way; **le chemin de fer** railway
la chemise shirt
le chèque cheque
le chéquier cheque-book
cher (f: chère) dear, or expensive
chercher to look for
le cheval horse; **le hamburger/ steak à cheval** hamburger/steak with an egg on top
les cheveux [m] hair
la cheville ankle
la chèvre goat
chez (at) the home/place of; **chez moi** (at) my place
chic posh, or elegant, or nice
le chien dog
les chips [f] crisps
le choc shock
le chocolat chocolate
le choeur choir
choisir to choose
le choix choice
le chômage unemployment; **au chômage** unemployed, or on the dole
le chômeur (f: la chômeuse) unemployed person
la chose thing
la choucroute sauerkraut
chouette* nice, or great
le chou-fleur cauliflower
chrétien(ne) Christian
chuchoter to whisper
le cidre cider
le ciel sky
la cigarette cigarette
le cil eyelash
le cimetière cemetery
le cinéma or **le ciné*** cinema
cinglé(e)* crazy
la circulation traffic
circuler to move (along)
les ciseaux [m] scissors
le citron lemon; **le citron pressé** drink of freshly squeezed lemon juice with sugar and water
le clafoutis desert of fruit cooked in batter
clair(e) clear, or light
la clarinette clarinet
classique classical
la clé key, or spanner; **la clé anglaise** adjustable spanner
le/la client(e) customer
le clignotant indicator
climatisé(e) air-conditioned
la clope** cigarette
le clou nail
le cochon pig
le coeur heart; **avoir le coeur brisé** to be heart-broken; **avoir mal au coeur** to feel sick/queasy
le coffre (car) boot; **le coffre-fort** safe (box for valuables)
se cogner (contre) to bump into, or to hit
le coiffeur (f: la coiffeuse) hairdresser
la coiffure hairstyle
le coin corner; **du coin*** local
coincé(e) stuck, or (slang) uptight
le col collar, or (mountain) pass
la colère anger; **en colère** angry
le colis parcel
le collant leotard, or tights
collectionner to collect
le collège secondary/high school
le collier necklace
la colline hill
la colonie de vacances children's summer camp
le combat fight
combien? how many/much?
la combinaison overalls, or wetsuit, or ski suit
le combiné (phone) receiver
la comédie comedy; **jouer la comédie** to put on an act
la commande order, or controls
commander to order
comme like, or as
comment how
les commérages [m] gossip
la commère gossip (a person)
la compagnie company; **la compagnie aérienne** airline
le compas compass
complet (f: complète) full, or booked up
composter to stamp, or to punch (a hole)
le composteur man/machine that punches hole in ticket
comprendre to understand
le comprimé pill, or tablet
compris(e) understood, or included
le comptoir counter
le concert concert
le concombre cucumber
le concours contest, or exam
conduire to drive
la confiance trust
la confiserie confectionery, confectioner's (shop)
la confiture jam
confondre to mix up, or to confuse
confortable comfortable
le congélateur freezer
connaître to know
connu(e) known, or well-known
le conseil advice
la consigne (de bagages) left-luggage office
constipé(e) constipated
le consulat consulate

contagieux (f: contagieuse) contagious
content(e) happy, or pleased
le contraceptif contraceptive
le/la contractuel(le) traffic warden
le contraire opposite
contrarié(e) upset, or annoyed
contre against
le contrôle test, or inspection
contrôler to control, or to inspect
le contrôleur (f: la contrôleuse) ticket inspector
cool* cool, or fab
le copain* (f: la copine*) friend
copier to copy
le coquetier eggcup
les coquillages [m] shellfish
la coquille shell
le cor horn
la corde rope
le corps body
correct(e) correct
la correspondance (trains, planes) connection
le/la correspondant(e) pen pal
la Corse Corsica
cosmopolite cosmopolitan
le costume suit, or costume
la côte coast
le côté side; **à côté de** next to
la côtelette (food) chop
le coton cotton, or cotton wool
le cou neck
coucher to sleep, or to spend the night
se coucher to go to bed
le coucher du soleil sunset
la couchette sleeper, or berth
le coude elbow
la couette duvet
la couleur colour
le coup blow, or shock; **le coup d'envoi** kick-off; **le coup de fil** phone call; **le coup de main** (helping) hand; **le coup de pied** kick; **le coup de poing** punch; **le coup de soleil** sunburn
coupable guilty
la coupe cut, or (ice cream) dish; **la Coupe du monde** World Cup
couper to cut
le courage courage; **courage!** cheer up!
courageux (f: courageuse) brave, or courageous
couramment fluently, or commonly
courant(e) common; **être au courant de** to know about
la courbature ache; **avoir des courbatures** to be stiff
courir to run
le courrier post, or mail
le cours course, or lesson
la course race, or errand
les courses [f] shopping
court(e) short
le/la cousin(e) cousin
le couteau knife
coûter to cost
la coutume custom
couvert(e) covered; **c'est couvert** (weather) it's overcast
la couverture blanket, or cover
crade** scruffy
craindre to fear
le crampon (on boot) stud
craquer to crackle, or (slang) to crack up, or to lose it
la cravache (riding) whip
la cravate tie
le crawl (swimming) crawl
le crayon pencil
la crème cream; **le (grand) crème** (large) coffee with milk/cream; **la crème anglaise** custard; **la crème patissière** confectioner's custard; **la crème solaire** sun cream
la crêpe pancake
crevé(e)** exhausted, or shattered
crever to burst, or to puncture
la crevette prawn
crier to scream, or to shout
la crinière mane
la crise fit, or crisis
critiquer to criticize
croire to believe
la croix cross
le croque-madame ham and cheese toasted sandwich with an egg on top
le croque-monsieur ham and cheese toasted sandwich
le crottin small goat's cheese
cru(e) raw
les crudités [f] dish of salad and/ or raw vegetables
la cuillère spoon
le cuir leather
la cuisine kitchen
le cuisinier cook
la cuisinière cook, or stove
le culot* cheek, or nerve
culturel(le) cultural
curieux (f: curieuse) curious, or odd, or nosy

d'abord first
d'accord OK, or all right; **être d'accord** to agree
la dame lady
dangereux (f: dangereuse) dangerous
dans in
danser to dance
le danseur (f: la danseuse) dancer
la date (calendar) date
de from, or of
le dé dice, or thimble
se débarrasser de to get rid of
débile** stupid, or feeble-minded
debout standing
se débrouiller to cope
le début start, or beginning
le/la débutant(e) beginner
le déca* a decaff. coffee
décaféiné(e) decaffeinated
la décapotable open top car
le décapsuleur bottle opener
décembre December
les déchets [m] rubbish
déchirer to rip
décider to decide
décoller (plane) to take off
décolleté(e) low-cut
décontracté(e) casual, or relaxed, or laid-back
le découvert overdraft
découvrir to discover
décrire to describe
déçu(e) disappointed
défendu(e) forbidden
la défense defence; **défense d'entrer/de fumer** no entry/ smoking; **la défense de l'environnement** environmental conservation
définir to define
déglinguer** to bust, or to fall to pieces
dégonflé(e) (tyre) flat, or (slang) chicken (cowardly)
dégoûtant(e) disgusting
dégoûter to disgust
dégueulasse** revolting, or gross
la dégustation tasting
déjà already
déjeuner to have lunch
le déjeuner lunch; **le petit déjeuner** or **le petit déj*** breakfast
délicieux (f: délicieuse) delicious

délirer to be delirious; **tu délires*!** you must be out of your mind!
demain tomorrow; **après-demain** the day after tomorrow
demander to ask
se demander to wonder
le démaquillant make-up remover
déménager to move house
dément(e)* fab, or cool
demi(e) half; **il est dix heures et demie** it's half past ten; **le demi-frère** stepbrother, or half-brother; **la demi-soeur** stepsister, or half-sister; **le demi-tarif** half-price
le demi-tour U-turn;
la demi-bouteille half-bottle
la démocratie democracy
démodé(e) old-fashioned
démolir to demolish, or to wreck
la dent tooth
le dentifrice toothpaste
le/la dentiste dentist
le déodorant deodorant
le départ departure
dépasser to exceed, or to overtake
se dépêcher to hurry
dépendre to depend
dépenser to spend
déposer to drop off
déprimant(e) depressing
déprimé(e) depressed
depuis since, or for
déranger to disturb;
ça te/vous dérange? do you mind?
le dériveur sailing dinghy
le dernier (f: la dernière) last, or latest
derrière behind
le derrière bottom
des some, or of the, or any
désagréable unpleasant
descendre to go/walk down, or to get off
se déshabiller to undress
désolé(e) sorry, or desolate
le désordre mess
le dessert dessert
le dessin picture, or drawing; **le dessin animé** cartoon
dessiner to draw
dessus above, or on top
le détail detail
le détendeur (diving) regulator
se détendre to relax
détester to hate
le détour detour
devant in front of
devenir to become
deviner to guess
devoir to have to, or to owe
les devoirs [m] homework
diabétique diabetic
le dialecte dialect
la diarrhée diarrhoea
le dictionnaire or **le dico*** dictionary
le dieu god
différent(e) different
difficile difficult
dimanche Sunday
le diminutif shortened name
la dinde turkey
le dîner supper
dingue* crazy
diplomatique diplomatic, or tactful
dire to say, or to tell;
ça te dit de...? would you like to...?
direct(e) direct; **en direct** live
la direction direction
la discussion discussion, or examination
discuter to discuss, or to argue
disparaître to disappear
la dispute argument
se disputer to quarrel
le disquaire music store
le distributeur distributor; **le distributeur (automatique)** vending machine; **le distributeur (automatique) de billets** cash dispenser, or ticket machine
divorcé(e) divorced
le docteur doctor
le doigt finger
le dollar dollar
le dommage harm, or damage;
quel dommage! what a shame!
donner to give
dormir to sleep; **dormir à la belle étoile** to sleep out under the stars
le dortoir dormitory
le dos back; **le dos crawlé** (swimming) backstroke, or back crawl
la douane customs
double double
doubler to double, or to dub, or to overtake
douce (see 'doux')
la douche shower
la doudoune* puffa jacket
doué(e) talented
doux (f: douce) soft, or sweet
draguer** to flirt, or to chat/ pick up
le dragueur**
(f: la dragueuse)** flirt
le drap sheet
la drogue drug
le/la drogué(e) drug addict
droit(e) straight; **tout droit** straight ahead
le droit law, or right;
avoir le droit to be allowed;
les droits de l'homme [m] human rights
la droite right
drôle funny
du some, or of the, or any
les dunes [f] dunes
dur(e) hard, or difficult

l'eau [f] water; **l'eau (minérale) plate/gazeuse** still/sparkling (mineral) water
éblouir to dazzle
l'échange [m] exchange
échanger to exchange, or to swap
s'échapper to escape
l'écharpe [f] scarf
s'échauffer to warm up
les échecs [m] chess
l'échelle ladder
échouer to fail
éclater to explode; **éclater de rire** to burst out laughing
l'école [f] school; **l'école des beaux-arts** art school
l'écologie [f] ecology
écossais(e) Scottish
l'Écosse [f] Scotland
l'écoute [f] (sailing) sheet
écouter to listen
les écouteurs [m] earphones
l'écran [m] screen; **l'écran total [m]** sun block
écrire to write
l'écrivain [m] writer
l'éducation [f] education
effacer to rub out
effrayant(e) scary
égal(e) equal; **ça m'est égal!** I don't care!
l'église [f] church
égoïste selfish
l'élastique [m] elastic, or rubber band
électrique electric
l'élection [f] election
elle she, or her

l'embarquement [m] boarding; **la salle d'embarquement** departure lounge
embêtant(e) annoying
l'embouteillage [m] traffic jam
embrasser to kiss
embrouiller to muddle, or to confuse
l'émission [f] programme (on TV/radio)
emmener to take
empêcher to prevent
emporter to take, or to take away; **les plats à emporter [m]** take-away dishes
emprunter to borrow
enceinte pregnant
encore again, or still; **encore un peu** a little more; **pas encore** not yet
l'endroit [m] place
énervant(e) annoying
énerver to annoy
l'enfant [m/f] child
l'enfer [m] hell
enfin at last
enflé(e) swollen
s'enfuir to run away
engueuler** to tell off
s'engueuler** to have a row
enlever to take off
les ennuis [m] trouble, or problems
s'ennuyer to be bored
ennuyeux (f: ennuyeuse) boring, or annoying, or worrying
enregistré(e) (luggage) checked in, or (post) registered
l'enregistrement [m] check-in
enregistrer to record, or (luggage) to check in
enrhumé(e): être enrhumé(e) to have a cold
enseigner to teach
ensemble together
ensoleillé(e) sunny
entendre to hear
s'entendre to get on/along
entendu understood, or fine
entier (f: entière) whole
l'entorse [f] sprain
l'entracte [m] interval, or intermission
s'entraîner to train
entre between
l'entrecôte [f] type of steak
l'entrée [f] entrance, or first course, or main course; **entrée libre** free admission
entrer to come/go in
l'entretien [m] interview, or upkeep
l'enveloppe [f] envelope
l'envers [m] wrong side; **à l'envers** inside out, or upside-down
environ approximately, or about
l'environnement [m] environment
envoyer to send
épais(se) thick
l'épaule [f] shoulder
l'épaulière [f] shoulder pad
épicé(e) hot, or spicy
l'épice [f] spice
les épinards [m] spinach
l'épingle [f] pin; **l'épingle de sûreté** safety pin
l'éponge [f] sponge
épouvantable dreadful
épuisé(e) exhausted
l'équipe [f] team
l'équitation [f] riding
l'erreur [f] mistake
l'escalade [f] climbing
escalader to climb
l'escale [f] stopover
l'escalier [m] stairs; **l'escalier roulant (m)** escalator
l'escargot [m] snail
l'espace [m] space
l'Espagne [f] Spain
espérer to hope
l'esprit [m] spirit; **l'esprit mal tourné** dirty mind
l'essai [m] test, or attempt
essayer to try
l'essence [f] petrol; **l'essence sans plomb (f)** unleaded petrol
essoufflé(e) out of breath
l'essuie-glace [m] windscreen wiper
l'essuie-tout [m] kitchen paper
l'est [m] east
est-ce que... ? see Questions p.45
l'estomac [m] stomach
et and
l'étage [m] floor (level)
l'étagère [f] shelf
les États-Unis [m] United States
l'été [m] summer
éteindre to switch off
éteint(e) (switched) off
éternuer to sneeze
l'étoile [f] star
étrange strange
l'étranger (f: l'étrangère) foreigner; **à l'étranger** abroad
être (see p. 45) to be
l'étrier [m] stirrup
étroit(e) narrow
les études [f] studies; **les études supérieures [f]** higher education
l'étudiant(e) [m/f] student
étudier to study
l'Europe [f] Europe
européen(ne) European
s'évanouir to faint
l'événement [m] event
évident(e) obvious
éviter to avoid
exact right, or correct
exagéré(e) exaggerated, or over the top
exagérer to exaggerate
l'examen [m] exam(ination)
l'excédent [m] surplus; **l'excédent de bagages [m]** excess baggage
excellent(e) excellent
excentrique eccentric
l'exception [f] exception, or odd one out
excité(e) excited
s'exciter to get excited
l'excursion [f] tour, or trip
excusez-moi excuse me
l'exercice [m] exercise
exotique exotic
l'expérience [f] experience, or experiment
expirer to run out, or to expire
expliquer to explain
exploser to explode or blow up
l'exposition [f] exhibition
exprès on purpose
l'express [m] espresso coffee, or fast train
l'extérieur [m] outside
extra* brilliant, or fab
extraordinaire extraordinary

fabriquer to make, or to manufacture
face: en face de opposite
fâché(e) cross, or angry
se fâcher to get cross/angry, or to fall out with
facile easy
la façon manner, or way
faible weak
la faiblesse weakness
la faim hunger; **avoir faim** to be hungry
faire (see p.45) to make, or to do

fait: il fait froid/beau it's cold/fine (weather)
la falaise cliff
la famille family
fantastique fantastic
farci(e) stuffed
le fard make-up; **le fard à joues** blusher; **le fard à paupières** eye shadow
fatigué(e) tired
fauché(e)** broke
la faute fault, or mistake
le fauteuil armchair; **le fauteuil roulant** wheelchair **faux (f: fausse)** false, or wrong
félicitations congratulations
le/la féministe feminist
la femme woman, or wife
la fenêtre window
la ferme farm
fermé(e) closed
fermer to close; **fermer à clé** to lock
la fermeture closure, or fastening; **la fermeture éclair** zip
la fête party; **faire la fête** to party; **la fête foraine** funfair
fêter to celebrate
le feu fire; **le feu d'artifice** fireworks; **le feu rouge** traffic lights
la feuille leaf, or (paper) sheet
le feuilleton soap opera, or serial
les feux [m] lights; **les feux de signalisation** traffic lights
février February
la ficelle string
ficher* to do, or to put; **fiche-moi la paix!*** leave me alone!; **fiche le camp!*** get lost!
se ficher de* not to give a damn
fidèle faithful
fier (f: fière) proud
la fièvre fever
le fil thread
la fille girl, or daughter
le film film
le fils son
la fin end
finir to finish
la fixation (ski) binding
fixer to fix (a date/price), or to stare
la flaque d'eau puddle
le flash (camera) flash
la fléchette dart
la fleur flower
le fleuve (large) river
le flic** cop
le flingue** gun
le flipper pinball
flipper** to flip (to become excited/depressed/scared)
flotter to float, or (slang) to rain
la flûte flute
le foc (sailing) jib
le foie liver; **le foie gras** rich goose or duck liver pâté
la fois time, or occasion
folle (see 'fou')
la folle mad woman
foncé(e) dark
le fond bottom, or back (of throat/room etc.); **le fond de teint** foundation (make-up)
fondre to melt; **fondre en larmes** to burst into tears
la fondue (savoyarde) dish of hot melted cheese with bread; **la fondue bourguignonne** thin strips of meat cooked at table
la fontaine fountain
le football or **le foot*** football; **le football américain** American football
le footballeur (f: la footballeuse) football player
le footing jogging
la forêt forest
le forfait set price, or (ski) lift pass
la formation training
la forme shape; **en forme** fit, or well
former to train
formidable wonderful, or terrific
fort(e) loud, or strong
fou (f: folle) mad, or crazy
le fou madman
la foudre lightning
le foulard scarf
la foule crowd
le four oven
la fourchette fork
la fourmi ant
frais (f: fraîche) fresh, or chilled
la fraise strawberry
la framboise raspberry
français(e) French
la France France
le frangin* brother
la frangine* sister
frapper to hit, or to knock
le frein brake
le frère brother
le fric* dosh (money)
le frigo fridge
frileux (f: frileuse) sensitive to the cold
frimer* to boast, or to show off
les fringues* [f] clothes
le frisbee frisbee
frisé(e) very curly
la frisée type of lettuce with very curly leaves
le frisson shiver, or thrill
frit(e) fried
les frites [f] chips, or French fries
froid(e) cold
le fromage cheese
la frontière border, or frontier
le fruit fruit
les fruits de mer [m] seafood
fumer to smoke
le fumeur (f: la fumeuse) smoker
fumeurs smoking; **non-fumeurs** non-smoking
furax** livid, or furious
le fuseau (de ski) ski pants

gâcher to spoil
la gaffe* blunder; **faire gaffe*** to watch out; **faire une gaffe*** to put your foot in it
gaffer* to blunder, or to put your foot in it
le/la gagnant(e) winner
gagner to win, or to earn
la galère: **quelle galère*!** what a mess/disaster!
la galerie gallery, or roof rack
gallois(e) Welsh
le gant glove
le garçon boy, or waiter
garder to keep, or to look after
le/la gardien(ne) guard, or caretaker; **le gardien de but** goalkeeper
la gare railway station; la **gare routière** bus station
se garer to park
le gars* guy
le gaspillage waste
gaspiller to waste
gâté(e) spoiled
le gâteau cake
la gauche left
le gaz gas
gazeux (f: gazeuse) fizzy
le gazole diesel
le gel gel, or frost
geler to freeze
Gémeaux (star sign) Gemini
gênant(e) embarrassing, or a nuisance

le gendarme police officer
gêner to bother, or to be/get in the way
génial(e) inspired, or brilliant, or great
le genou knee
le genre type, or gender
les gens [m/f] people
gentil(le) kind, or nice
la géographie geography
le gigot d'agneau leg of lamb
le gilet cardigan, or waistcoat; **le gilet de sauvetage** life jacket; **le gilet stabilisateur** (diving) buoyancy aid
le gingembre ginger
le gîte house for rent in the countryside
la glace ice, or ice cream, or mirror
la glacière cool box
le glaçon ice cube
glisser to slip, or to slide
le goal* goalie
la godasse** shoe
gonflable inflatable
gonflé(e) swollen, or (slang) cheeky
la gorge throat
la gourde water bottle, or flask
gourmand(e) greedy
la gourmette chain bracelet
le goût taste, or flavour
goûter to taste
le goûter tea (afternoon snack)
la goutte drop; **la goutte de pluie** raindrop
le gouvernail rudder, or helm
le gouvernement government
le gramme gram
grand(e) big, or tall, or large
la grand-mère grandmother
le grand-père grandfather
la Grande-Bretagne Britain
grandir to grow
le gras fat
gratter to scratch
gratuit(e) free
la Grèce Greece
le grenier attic
la grenouille frog
la grève strike
la grille iron gate, or grid, or (American football) facemask
grillé(e) grilled, or toasted
la grimpe* (rock) climbing
grimper to climb
le grimpeur (f: la grimpeuse) (rock) climber
la grippe flu
gris(e) grey
gros(se) large, or fat
grossier (f: grossière) rude, or crude
grossir to get fat, or to put on weight
la grotte cave
le groupe group, or band
la guêpe wasp
la guerre war
la gueule mouth (animal); **la gueule de bois*** hangover
le guichet ticket office, or (bank) counter
le/la guide guide
le guidon handlebars
la guitare guitar
le/la guitariste guitarist
le gymnase gymnasium
la gymnastique or **la gym*** gymnastics, or excercise classes

s'habiller to get dressed
habiter to live
l'habitude [f] habit; **d'habitude** usually; **comme d'habitude** as usual; **avoir l'habitude de** to be used to
habituel(le) usual
haïr to loathe
l'haleine [f] breath
le hamac hammock
handicapé(e) disabled
le haricot bean
le hasard chance
haut(e) high
le haut top; **en haut upstairs;** le **haut-parleur** loudspeaker
le hautbois oboe
l'hélicoptère [m] helicopter
l'herbe [f] grass
l'héroïne [f] heroine
le héros hero
hésiter to hesitate
l'heure [f] hour, or time; **à l'heure** on time; **les heures de pointe/d'affluence** rush hour; **quelle heure est-il?** what time is it?; **trois heures** three o'clock
heureusement luckily
heureux (f: heureuse) happy
le hibou owl
hier yesterday
hindou(e) Hindu
l'histoire [f] story, or history
l'hiver [m] winter
l'homme [m] man
homosexuel(le) or **homo*** homosexual
honnête honest
la honte shame; **quelle honte!** how embarrassing!
l'hôpital [m] hospital
le hoquet hiccups
l'horaire [m] timetable
l'horoscope [m] horoscope
l'horreur [f] horror; **avoir horreur de** to hate
horrible horrible
le hors-d'oeuvre [m] first course, or starter
hors de out of; **hors-jeu** offside; **hors-piste** off piste; **hors saison** off season; **hors taxe** duty-free
l'hôte [m] host, or **[m/f]** guest
l'hôtel [m] hotel; **l'hôtel de ville** town hall
l'hôtesse [f] hostess; **l'hôtesse de l'air** (female) flight attendant
l'huile [f] oil
l'huître [f] oyster
humain(e) human
l'humeur [f] mood; **de bonne/ mauvaise humeur** in a good/ bad mood
l'humour [m] humour
hurler to yell
hyper* extremely
l'hypocrite [m/f] hypocrite

ici here; **par ici** over here
l'idée [f] idea; **l'idée fixe** obsession
l'idiot(e) [m/f] idiot; **faire l'idiot(e)*** to act stupid
ignoble vile
il he, or it
l'île [f] island; **les îles anglo-normandes** the Channel Islands
il y a there is/are, or ago
l'immigré(e) [m/f] immigrant
immobile still
imperméable waterproof
l'imperméable or **l'imper* [m]** raincoat
impoli(e) rude
important(e) important
importé(e) imported
impossible impossible
impressionnant(e) impressive
l'imprimante [f] printer
l'inconvénient [m] drawback, or disadvantage
incroyable unbelievable
l'Inde [f] India

l'indicatif [m] area code
l'indigestion [f] upset stomach
indiquer to point, or to show
indispensable essential, or vital
l'infirmier (f: l'infirmière) nurse
les informations or **les info*** [f] news, or information
l'informatique [f] computing
l'infusion [f] herb tea
injuste unfair, or wrong
inquiet (f: inquiète) worried
s'inquiéter to worry
s'inscrire to join, or to sign up for, or to register
l'insolation [f] sunstroke
installer to install, or put in
l'instant [m] moment; **à l'instant** now
l'instrument [m] instrument
l'insulte [f] insult
insupportable unbearable
intelligent(e) intelligent
l'intention [f] intention; **avoir l'intention de** to mean to
interdit(e) forbidden
intéressant(e) interesting
s'intéresser à to be interested in
l'intérieur [m] inside
l'interphone [m] intercom
introduire to insert
inutile useless
l'invitation [f] invitation
l'invité(e) [m/f] guest
inviter to invite, or to ask out
irlandais(e) Irish
l'Irlande [f] Ireland
isolé(e) isolated
l'Italie [f] Italy
l'itinéraire [m] route

jaloux (f: jalouse) jealous
jamais never
la jambe leg
le jambon ham
janvier January
le jardin garden; **le jardin public** park
jaune yellow
le jaune (d'oeuf) (egg) yolk
je (or j') I
le jean jeans; **en jean** (made of) denim
jeter to throw, or to throw away/out
le jeu game, or quiz; **les jeux vidéos** video games; **la salle de jeux vidéos** (amusement) arcade
jeudi Thursday
jeune young
les jodhpurs [m] jodhpurs
le jogging jogging
joli(e) pretty
la joue cheek
jouer to play
le jouet toy
le joueur (f: la joueuse) player
le jour day; **le jour de congé** day off; **le jour férié** national holiday; **à jour** up-to-date
le journal newspaper, or personal diary
le/la journaliste journalist
la journée day, or daytime
joyeux (f: joyeuse) happy, or cheerful
juif (f: juive) Jewish
juillet July
juin June
le jumeau twin (brother)
la jumelle twin (sister)
les jumelles [f] binoculars
la jupe skirt
jurer to swear
le jus juice
jusqu'à until
juste fair, or just

kascher kosher
le kayak canoe, or kayak
le kilo kilo
le kilomètre kilometre
le kiosque news stand
le kir white wine with blackcurrant; **le kir royal** champagne with blackcurrant
le klaxon horn

la (or l') the, or her, or it
là there; **là-bas** over there
le lac lake
le/la lâche coward
lâcher to let go
laid(e) ugly
la laine wool
laisser to leave, or to let; **laisser tomber** to drop, or to let go, or (slang) to let down, or stand (someone) up; **laisser tranquille** to leave alone
le laissez-passer (entry) pass
le lait milk
le laitue lettuce
la lame blade
la lampe lamp, or light; **la lampe de poche** torch
lancer to throw
la langue language, or tongue
le lapin rabbit
les lardons [m] small pieces of bacon
la laque hair-spray
laquelle which (one)
large wide
la larme tear
la latte (sailing) batten
le lavabo wash basin
le lave-linge washing machine
laver to wash
le lave-vaisselle dishwasher
se laver to wash (yourself)
la laverie launderette
le (or l') the, or him, or it
le lèche-vitrines window shopping
le lecteur de DVD DVD player
léger (f: légère) light
le légume vegetable
le lendemain the next day
lent(e) slow
la lentille lentil; **la lentille (de contact)** contact lens; **la lentille souple/dure** soft/hard contact lens
lequel which (one)
les the, or them
la lessive washing powder, or laundry
la lettre letter
leur their, or them
se lever to get up
la lèvre lip
la librairie bookshop
libre free
la licence degree
le lieu place; **au lieu de** instead of
la ligne line
le linge washing, or linen (sheets etc.)
Lion (star sign) Leo
lire to read
le lit bed; **le grand lit** double bed
le litre litre
la littérature literature
le livre book; **le livre de poche** paperback book
la livre (sterling) pound
location (de) for hire/rent
la locomotive (train) engine
le logement accommodation
loger (quelqu'un) to put (someone) up
le logiciel software
loin far
les loisirs [m] leisure, or free time

long(ue) long
longtemps a long time
louche dodgy, or dubious
louer to rent, or to hire
lourd(e) heavy
la luge toboggan
lui him, or her, or it
la lumière light
lundi Monday
la lune moon
les lunettes [f] glasses; **les lunettes de soleil** sunglasses; **les lunettes de ski** ski goggles
le lycée secondary/high school

ma my
le machin* thing
la machine machine
macho* macho
madame Mrs, or madam
mademoiselle Miss
le magasin shop; **le grand magasin** department store; **faire les magasins** to go around the shops
la magnésie chalk (for climbing); **le sac à magnésie** chalk bag
mai May
maigrir to get thin, or to lose weight
le maillet mallet
le maillot swimming trunks, or swimsuit, or team shirt/jersey; **le maillot deux-pièces** bikini; **le maillot une pièce** one piece swimsuit
la main hand
maintenant now
la mairie town hall
mais but
la maison house, or home
mal bad, or wrong, or badly; **avoir mal** to hurt; **avoir mal à la tête/aux dents** to have a headache/toothache; **le mal de mer** seasickness; **le mal du pays** homesickness
malade ill, or sick
malheureusement unfortunately
malheureux (f: malheureuse) unhappy, or upset
malin (f: maligne) cunning, or clever (smart)
la manche sleeve; **la Manche** the Channel; **le tunnel sous la Manche** the Channel tunnel
manger to eat
la manifestation or **la manif*** demonstration
le mannequin (fashion) model
manquer to miss
le manteau coat
le maquillage make-up
le marchand stallholder, or salesman; **le marchand de journaux** newsagent; **le marchand de fruits et légumes** greengrocer
marchander to bargain
la marche step, or (sport) walking; **faire marche arrière** to reverse
le marché market; **le marché aux puces** flea market
marcher to walk, or to be in working order; **faire marcher quelqu'un*** to have someone on
mardi Tuesday
la marée tide
la margarine margarine
le mari husband
le mariage wedding
le Maroc Morocco
marquer to mark; **marquer un but/un point** to score a goal/ point
marrant(e)* fun, or funny
marre*: en avoir marre* to be fed up
se marrer* to have a laugh
marron brown
le marron chestnut
mars March
le marteau hammer
le mascara mascara
le masque mask
le mât mast
le match match, or game; **le match à domicile** home match/ game
le matelas mattress; **le matelas pneumatique** air bed
le matelot sailor
le matériel kit, or equipment
le matin morning
la matinée morning, or afternoon performance; **faire la grasse matinée** to sleep in late
mauvais(e) bad
le mazout (fuel) oil
le mec* guy, bloke
le/la mécanicien(ne) mechanic or train driver
méchant(e) wicked, or naughty
le médecin doctor
la médecine medicine (the science)
les médias [m] media
le médicament medicine (medication)
la Méditerranée the Mediterranean
la méduse jellyfish
meilleur(e) better
le/la meilleur(e) best
mélanger to mix
le melon melon
le/la même same
la menace threat
le/la mendiant(e) beggar
le meneur (f: la meneuse) leader, or cheerleader
le mensonge lie, or fib
le menteur (f: la menteuse) liar
mentir to lie
le menu set menu
la mer sea
merci thank you
mercredi Wednesday
la mère mother
merveilleux (f: merveilleuse) wonderful
messieurs gentlemen
la météo weather forecast
le mètre metre
le métro underground, or tube
le metteur en scène (play) director
mettre to put, or to put on
le meurtre murder
le micro microphone
le micro-ondes microwave
le microbe bug
midi midday, or noon
le miel honey
le/la mien(ne) mine
mieux better; **se sentir mieux** to feel better; **il vaut mieux...** it is better to...
le/la mieux best
mignon(ne) sweet, **or** cute
le milieu middle, or environment
le millefeuille cream slice
mi-longs (cheveux) shoulder length (hair)
minable* pathetic
mince thin; **mince!*** damn!
la minette* babe (girl)
mineur(e) under age
minuit midnight
le miroir mirror
mixte mixed, or (school) co-ed
la mobylette moped

moche* lousy, or ugly
la mode fashion; **à la mode** fashionable
le mode method; **le mode de vie** lifestyle; **le mode d'emploi** user instructions
moi me
le moineau or le piaf* sparrow
moins less; **au moins** at least; **huit heures moins dix** ten to eight; **une heure moins le quart** a quarter to one
le mois month
la moitié half
molle (see 'mou')
mon my
le monde world
le moniteur/la monitrice instructor
la monnaie money, or change
le monokini bikini bottoms
le monoski monoski
monsieur Mr, or Sir
monstrueux (f: monstrueuse) outrageous
la montagne mountain
le montant total amount
monter to go/walk up
la montre watch
montrer to show
le monument monument
se moquer de to make fun of
le moral morale; **remonter le moral à quelqu'un** to cheer someone up
le morceau piece
mordre to bite
mordu(e)* de madly in love with, or mad about
le mors (riding) bit
mort(e) dead
la morue cod
la mosquée mosque
le mot word; **le gros mot** swearword; **les mots croisés [m]** crossword
le motard biker, or police on motorbike
le motif pattern, or motive
la moto motorbike
mou (f: molle) soft
la mouche fly
le mouchoir handkerchief
mouillé(e) wet
la moule mussel; **moules marinières** mussels in white wine
le moulin à vent windmill
mourir to die
la mousse foam, or mousse
le moustique mosquito
la moutarde mustard
le mouton sheep
moyen(ne) average, or medium
le mur wall
mûr(e) mature, or ripe
le muscle muscle
la musculation gym (with weights)
le musée museum
le/la musicien(ne) musician
la musique music
musulman(e) Muslim
myope short-sighted

nager to swim
naïf (f: naïve) naïve
la naissance birth; **la date de naissance** date of birth
la nana** girl
la natation swimming
la nationalité nationality
nature plain
la nature nature
le navet turnip
naturel(le) natural
navré(e) terribly sorry, or distressed
naze** exhausted
ne... pas not (see also Negatives p. 45)
nécessaire necessary
la neige snow
neiger to snow
le nerf nerve; **taper sur les nerfs* (de quelqu'un)** to get on (someone's) nerves
le nez nose
n'importe it doesn't matter; **n'importe quel(le)** any; **n'importe qui** anyone; **n'importe quoi** anything, or (slang) nonsense
le niveau level or standard
Noël Christmas
noir(e) black; **il fait noir** it is dark; **broyer du noir** to be down in the dumps
la noisette hazelnut
la noix walnut; **la noix de cajou** cashew nut; **la noix de coco** coconut; **la noix du Brésil** brazil nut
le nom name; **le nom de famille** last name
non no
le nord north
nos our
la note note, or mark, or bill
notre our
nouer to knot, or to tie
les nouilles [f] noodles
la nourriture food
nous we, or us
nouveau (f: nouvelle) new; **de nouveau** again; **le nouvel an** new year; **la Nouvelle-Zélande** New Zealand
nouvel(le) (see 'nouveau')
les nouvelles [f] news
novembre November
nu(e) naked
le nuage cloud
la nuit night
nul(le) nil, or lousy, or naff; **nulle part** nowhere; **le match nul** draw (equal score)
le numéro number

l'objectif [m] (camera) lens
l'objet [m] object; **les objets trouvés** lost-property
obligatoire compulsory
l'occasion [f] opportunity; **d'occasion** second-hand
occupé(e) busy, or (toilet) engaged
s'occuper de to take care of, or to take charge of
octobre October
l'odeur [f] smell
odieux (f: odieuse) obnoxious
l'oeil [m] eye
l'oeuf [m] egg; **l'oeuf à la coque** soft-boiled egg; **l'oeuf au plat** fried egg; **les oeufs brouillés** scrambled eggs; **l'oeuf dur** hard-boiled egg; **l'oeuf poché** poached egg; **les oeufs à la neige** dessert of whipped egg whites in custard
officiel(le) official
offrir to offer
l'oignon [m] onion
l'oiseau [m] bird
l'olive [f] olive
l'ombre [f] shade
l'omelette [f] omelette
on we, or people e.g. **on dit que...** people say that...
l'oncle [m] uncle
l'opticien(ne) [m/f] optician
optimiste optimistic
l'orage [m] thunderstorm
l'orange [f] orange
l'orchestre [m] orchestra
ordinaire ordinary
l'ordinateur [m] computer
l'ordre [m] order
les ordures [f] rubbish

l'oreille [f] ear
l'oreiller [m] pillow
organiser to organize
l'organisme de charité [m] charity organization
original(e) offbeat, or original
l'os [m] bone
oser to dare
ou or
où where
oublier to forget
l'ouest [m] west
oui yes
l'outil [m] tool
ouvert(e) open
l'ouvre-boîte [m] can opener
l'ouvre-bouteille [m] bottle opener
ouvrir to open

la pagaille* mess, or chaos
la page page
le pain bread; **le petit pain** bread roll; **le pain complet** wholemeal bread; **le pain grillé** toast; **le pain au raisin** bun with raisins; **le pain au chocolat** like a croissant but with chocolate filling
la paix peace
le palais palace
la palme (diving) flipper
le/la pamplemousse grapefruit
le panaché shandy
le panier basket
la panique panic
la panne breakdown; **en panne** out of order, or broken down
le panneau sign
le pansement plaster
le pantalon trousers
la papeterie stationer's shop
le papier paper; **le papier hygiénique** toilet paper
les papiers documents
le papillon butterfly; **le papillon de nuit moth**
Pâques Easter
par by, or through
le parachute parachute
le parapluie umbrella
le parasol parasol
le paravent windbreak
le parc park; **le parc d'attractions** theme park
parce que because
pardon sorry, or excuse me; **demander pardon** to apologize
pardonner to forgive
le pare-battage (boat) fender
le pare-brise windscreen
les parents [m] parents
le pare-soleil (camera) lens hood
paresseux (f: paresseuse) lazy
parfait(e) perfect
le parfum perfume, or flavour
le parking car park
parler to speak, or to talk
la parole word
partager to share, or to split
le/la partenaire partner
le parti (political) party
participer to take part
particulier (f: particulière) particular, or private
la partie part; **la partie de cartes/tennis** game of cards/tennis
partir to leave, or to go away
partout everywhere
pas not (see Negatives p.45)
le pas footstep
le passage passage
le passager (f: la passagère) passenger
le passeport passport
passer to pass, or (film) to be on/showing
se passer to happen
la passerelle footbridge, or gangway
passionnant(e) exciting, or fascinating
le/la passionné(e) fan, or enthusiast
la pastèque watermelon
le pastis alcoholic drink tasting of aniseed
les pâtes [f] pasta
le patin skate, or skating; **le patin à glace** ice skate/ skating
la patinoire ice rink
la pâtisserie cake shop
le/la patron(ne) boss
la paupière eyelid
pauvre poor
la paye wage
payer to pay
le pays country, or nation; **le pays de Galles** Wales
le paysage scenery
PCV (phone) reversed charges
le péage toll
la peau skin
la pêche peach, or fishing; **avoir la pêche*** to be on top form
la pédale pedal; **perdre les pédales**** to get mixed up, or to lose your grip
le peigne comb
peindre to paint
la pellicule film (for camera)
la pelouse lawn; **pelouse interdite** keep off the grass
pendant during, or while
penser to think
la pension small hotel, or guest house; **pension complète** full board; **demi-pension** half board
le pépin pip
perdre to lose
perdu(e) lost
le père father
périmé(e) no longer valid
le périphérique ring road
le permis licence; **le permis de conduire** driving licence
le personnage character (in play/ cartoon/novel)
personne nobody
la personne person
la perte loss; **la perte de temps** waste of time
perturbé(e) disturbed
pessimiste pessimistic
la pétanque game of bowls played mostly in southern France
petit(e) small
les petits pois [m] peas
peu little, or not much
la peur fear
peut-être perhaps
le phare headlight, or lighthouse
la pharmacie chemist's shop or pharmacy
la philosophie or **la philo*** philosophy
la phobie phobia
la photo photo
le/la photographe photographer
le piano piano
le pichet jug, pitcher
la pièce coin, or play, or room; **la pièce de rechange** spare part
le pied foot; **pieds nus** barefoot
la pierre stone
le/la piéton(ne) pedestrian
piger** to catch on, or to get (a joke)
la pile battery; **jouer à pile ou face** to toss a coin
le pilote pilot
la pilule pill
la pince à épiler tweezers
le pinceau paintbrush
le ping-pong table tennis
le pin's pin badge

le pique-nique picnic
piquer to sting, or (slang) to nick (steal)
le piquet peg
la piqûre injection, or sting
pire worse
la piscine swimming pool
la pistache pistacchio
la piste track, or (ski) run
le placard cupboard
la place space, or seat, or (town) square
la plage beach
se plaindre to complain
plaire to please; **plaire à** to be fancied/liked by e.g. **elle plaît à Eric** Eric fancies her
plaisanter to joke
la plaisanterie joke
le plan plan, or map
la planche board; **la planche à voile** windsurfer (board); **la planche de surf** surf board
le/la planchiste windsurfer (person)
la plante plant
se planter** to get it all wrong, or to land yourself in it
plaquer** to chuck, or to dump (a girl/boyfriend)
le plastique plastic
plat(e) flat, or (water) still
le plat dish; **le plat du jour** dish of the day; **faire tout un plat**** to make a fuss
plein(e) full, or (slang) drunk; **faire le plein** to fill up
pleurer to cry
pleut: il pleut it's raining
pleuvoir to rain
plier to fold
le plomb lead
la plongée diving; la plongée **sous-marine** scuba diving
le plongeoir diving-board
plonger to dive
le plongeur (f: la plongeuse) diver
plouc** derogatory term meaning unsophisticated
la pluie rain
la plupart the majority
plus more
le pneu tyre
la poche pocket
la poêle frying pan or stove
le poème poem
le pognon** dosh (money)
le poids weight
la poignée handle
le poignet wrist
le poil hair (on body)
le point point, or dot;
à point (steak etc.) medium
la poire pear; **la poire belle Hélène** pear with vanilla ice cream and chocolate sauce
le poireau leek
le pois pea
le poisson fish
Poissons (star sign) Pisces
la poitrine chest, or breast
le poivre pepper
poli(e) polite
la police police
la politique politics
la pollution pollution
la pomme apple; **tomber dans les pommes*** to faint; **la pomme de terre** potato; **pommes de terre en robe des champs** baked/ jacket potatoes; **pommes vapeur** steamed potatoes
la pompe pump, or (slang) shoe
les pompiers [m] fire brigade
le pont bridge, or deck
populaire popular
le porc pork, or pig
le port harbour
la porte door, or (airport) gate
le portefeuille wallet
le porte-monnaie purse
porter to carry, or to wear
positif (f: positive) positive
possible possible
la poste, le bureau de poste post office
le pot jar, or pot, or (slang) luck; **prendre un pot*** to go for a drink; **pas de pot*** hard luck; **le pot-au-feu** meat and vegetable hotpot
potable drinkable; **non potable** not drinkable
le potage vegetable soup
la poubelle rubbish bin
la poule chicken, or hen
le poulet chicken
pour for
le pourboire tip
pourquoi why
pourri(e) rotten
pousser to push, or to grow; **pousse-toi!** move over!
pouvoir (see p.45) to be able to, or can
pratique practical
préféré(e) favourite
premier (f: première) first
prendre to take, or (food, drink) to have
le prénom first name
près de near; **tout près** close by
présenter to present, or to introduce (someone)
presque nearly
pressé(e) in a hurry; **le citron/ l'orange pressé(e)** drink of fresh lemon/orange
la pression pressure, or beer on tap
prêt(e) ready
prétentieux (f: prétentieuse) pretentious
prêter to lend
la preuve proof
principal(e) main
le printemps spring
la priorité right-of-way; **priorité à droite** give way to the right
pris(e) taken, or busy
la prise plug
la prison prison
privé(e) private
le prix price, or prize
probable probable, or likely
le problème problem
prochain(e) next
proche close
le professeur or **le/la prof*** teacher
profiter de to make the most of, or to take advantage of
profond(e) deep
le progrès progress
la promenade walk, or outing
se promener to walk about/ around, or to go for a walk
la promesse promise
proposer to suggest
propre clean
le/la propriétaire owner
protéger to protect
le provocateur (f: la provocatrice) trouble-maker
provoquer to cause trouble
prudent(e) careful
la prune plum
la pub* advertising, or publicity
le public audience
puer to stink
le pull-over or **le pull** sweater
pur(e) pure
la purée (de pomme de terre) mashed potato

le quai quay, or platform
la qualité quality
quand when
la quantité quantity
le quart quarter; **neuf heures et quart** quarter past nine
le quartier neighbourhood
que than, or that
quel(le) what, or which
quelque some, or any; **quelque chose** something; **quelques-un(e)s** a few
quelquefois sometimes
quelqu'un somebody
la quenelle a sort of light dumpling made of fish or meat
qu'est-ce que... ? what... ?; **qu'est ce-que c'est?** what is this/it?
la question question
la queue tail, or stalk, or queue; **faire la queue** to queue/line up
qui who
la quincaillerie hardware shop
quitter to leave; **ne quittez pas** (phone) hold the line
quoi what
quotidien(ne) daily

le raccourci short cut
raccrocher to hang up
raciste racist
la raclette dish of melted cheese with potatoes
raconter to tell (a story)
le radeau raft
le radiateur radiator
radin(e)* stingy
la radio radio
radoter* to waffle, or to babble
rafraîchir to cool down
le ragoût stew
raide steep, or stiff, or straight
le raisin grapes; **la grappe de raisin** bunch of grapes
la raison reason; **avoir raison** to be right
raisonnable sensible
ralentir to slow down
râler* to moan, or to complain
ramasser to pick up
la rame oar
ramer to row
lla randonnée walking, or hiking
ranger to put away
rapide fast, or quick
rappeler to remind, or to phone back
le rapport relationship
la raquette racket
rare unusual, or rare
ras le bol*: en avoir ras le bol* to be really fed up
se raser to shave
rasoir* boring
le rasoir razor
la ratatouille dish of aubergine, tomato and courgette
rater to miss, or (exam) to fail
rayé(e) striped
le rayon (in shop) shelf, or department
le réalisateur movie producer
la réception reception
la recette recipe
recevoir to receive
réchauffer to warm up
la recherche research
recommandé(e) (post) registered
recommander to recommend
se réconcilier to make up (become friends again)
reconnaissant(e) grateful
reconnaître to recognize
reculer to move backwards
réfléchir to think, reflect
la réduction discount
le réfrigérateur or **le frigo** fridge or refrigerator
regarder to look at, or to watch
le régime diet; **être au régime** to be on a diet
la région region, or area
la règle rule, or ruler
les règles [f] period (menstruation)
régulier (f: régulière) regular
le rein (part of body) kidney
les reins [m] small of the back; **avoir mal aux reins** to have backache
la religion religion
le remboursement refund
rembourser to pay back
remercier to thank
remettre to put back, or to postpone
les remparts [m] city walls
remplir to fill
remuer to stir
le renard fox
rencontrer to meet
le rendez-vous meeting, or appointment
rendre to give back; **ça me rend malade/jalous(e)/dingue*** it makes me ill/jealous/crazy
se rendre compte to realize
les rênes [f] (riding) reins
les renseignements [m] information
se renseigner to get information
la rentrée return, or beginning of term
réparer to repair
le repas meal
répéter to repeat, or to rehearse
la répétition rehearsal
le répondeur (automatique) answering machine
répondre to reply, or to answer
la réponse answer
le repos rest
se reposer to rest
la représentation performance
RER under/overground trains in and around Paris
la réservation reservation, or booking
réservé(e) reserved
réserver to reserve, or to book
le réservoir reservoir, or tank
respirer to breathe
ressembler (à) to look like
le restaurant or **le resto*** restaurant
le reste the rest
rester to stay
le résultat result
le retard delay; **en retard** late
le retour return
retourner to go back
le retrait withdrawal
la retraite retirement
retrouver to find, or to meet (up with)
réussir to succeed, or to pass (an exam)
le rêve dream
le réveil alarm clock
se réveiller to wake up
revenir to come back
le revers reverse (side), or (jacket) lapel, or (sleeve) cuff, or (trousers) turn up, or (tennis) backhand
revoir to see again
la revue magazine
le rez-de-chaussée ground floor
le rhume cold; **le rhume des foins** hayfever
riche rich
ridicule ridiculous
rien nothing; **de rien!** you're welcome! **ça ne fait rien!** it doesn't matter!

rigoler* to laugh, or to giggle
rigolo(te) funny
ringard(e)* old-fashioned
rire to laugh; **pour rire** for fun; **le fou rire** the giggles
le risque risk
la rivière river
le riz rice
la robe dress; **la robe de chambre** dressing gown
le robinet tap
la rocade bypass
le rocher boulder, or rock
le rock rock 'n roll
le rognon (food) kidney
les rollers roller skates
le roman novel
romantique romantic
rond(e) round, or plump
le rond-point roundabout
ronfler to snore
le roquefort strong blue cheese made from ewe's milk
rose pink
le rôti roast (meat)
la roue wheel
rouge red; **le rouge à lèvres** lipstick
rougir to blush
rouler to roll, or to go/drive (along)
le/la routard(e) backpacker
la route road
roux (f: rousse) (hair) red, or auburn
la rue street
les ruines [f] ruins
le rythme rhythm, or beat

sa her, or his
le sable sand
le sabot hoof
le sac bag; **le sac à dos** backpack; **le sac de couchage** sleeping bag
sacré(e) sacred, or (slang) really good, or damned
Sagittaire (star sign) Sagittarius
saignant(e) (steak etc.) rare
saigner to bleed
sain(e) healthy
saisir to grasp, or to get (understand)
la salade salad, or lettuce; **la salade composée** mixed salade; **la salade niçoise** olive, tomato and anchovy salad
sale dirty
salé(e) savoury, or salty
la salle room; **la salle à manger** dining room; **la salle d'attente** waiting room;
la salle de bain bathroom
le salon living room;
le salon de thé tea room
la salopette dungarees
salut bye, or hi
samedi Saturday
le sandwich sandwich
le sang blood
la sangle (riding) girth, or (climbing) sling
les sanitaires [m] wash rooms
sans without
les sans-abri [m/f] the homeless
la santé health; **en bonne santé** healthy; **santé!** cheers!
le sapin fir tree
sarcastique sarcastic
la sauce sauce
la saucisse sausage
le saucisson salami
sauf except
le saumon salmon
sauter to jump
sauvage wild
sauver to save
savoir to know
le savon soap
le saxophone or **le saxo*** saxophone
le/la saxophoniste saxophonist
scandaleux (f: scandaleuse) outrageous, or shocking
la scène scene, or stage
la science science
le score score
Scorpion (star sign) Scorpio
le scotch© adhesive tape
les SDF* [m/f] (sans domicile fixe) the homeless
la séance session, or showing (of a film/movie)
sec (f: sèche) dry;
à sec* broke
le sèche-cheveux hair-dryer
le sèche-linge tumble dryer
sécher to dry, or (slang) to bunk off
la seconde second
le secours help, or rescue; **au secours!** help! **les premiers secours [m]** first aid; **la roue de secours** spare wheel
le/la secrétaire secretary
la sécurité safety;
la ceinture de sécurité safety belt; **en sécurité** safe
séduire to seduce
séduisant(e) attractive
le sein breast
le séjour living room, or stay
le sel salt
le self-service or **le self*** self-service (restaurant)
la selle saddle; **le tapis de selle** saddle cloth
la semaine week
semblant: faire semblant to pretend
sembler to seem
le sens sense; **ça n'a pas de sens** it doesn't make sense; **le bon sens** common sense; **le sens unique** one-way street/system
sensationnel(le) or **sensass*** great, or fab
sensible sensitive
le sentier path
sentir to feel, or to smell
séparer to separate
septembre September
sérieux (f: sérieuse) serious
séropositif (f: séropositive) HIV positive
le serpent snake
serrer to tighten, or to hold tightly; **serrer (quelqu'un) dans ses bras** to hug (someone); **serrer la main** to shake hands
le serveur waiter
la serveuse waitress
le service service
la serviette towel, or napkin; **la serviette hygiénique** sanitary towel
servir to serve, or to wait on; **servir à** to be (used) for **se servir** to help yourself; **se servir de** to use
seul(e) alone, or lonely, or only
seulement only
le sexe sex
le shampooing shampoo
le short shorts
si if, or yes, or so, or such
le SIDA AIDS
le siècle century
le siège chair, or seat
siffler to whistle, or to boo
la signature signature
le signe sign
le silence silence
s'il te/vous plaît please
simple simple, or (ticket) single
sincère sincere, or truthful
sinon otherwise, or if not

le ski ski, or skiing; **le ski de fond** cross-country skiing;
le ski nautique water-skiing
skier to ski
le slip briefs, or knickers, or underpants
la SNCF French railways
la soeur sister
la soif thirst; **avoir soif** to be thirsty
soigné(e) neat; **peu soigné(e)** scruffy
soigner to look after
le soir evening; **ce soir** tonight; **hier soir** last night
le soldat soldier
soldé(e) reduced
les soldes [f] sales
le soleil sun
sombre dark
son his, or her
le son sound; **le son et lumière** sound and light show (takes place in historic locations on summer evenings)
sonner to ring
la sortie exit; **la sortie de secours** emergency exit
sortir to go out
le sou coin; **la machine à sous** slot machine
souffrir to suffer
souhaiter to wish, or to hope
soûl(e) drunk
le soulagement relief
se soûler to get drunk
la soupe soup
la source spring (source of water)
la sourcil eyebrow
sourd(e) deaf
le sourire smile
la souris mouse
sous under; **sous-marin(e)** underwater; **le sous-sol** basement; **le sous-titre** subtitle; **les sous-vêtements [m]** underwear
souterrain(e) underground
le soutien-gorge, or **le soutif**** bra
le souvenir souvenir
se souvenir de to remember
souvent often
la spécialité speciality
le spectacle show; **le guide des spectacles** entertainment guide
la spéléologie or **la spéléo*** caving
le spinnaker or **le spi** spinnaker
spontané(e) spontaneous
le sport sport
sportif (f: sportive) sporty
le stade stadium
le stage training course, or work experience
le stand-by stand-by
la station (metro) station;
la station-service petrol station;
la station de ski ski resort; **la station de taxis** taxi stand
le stationnement parking
la statue statue
le steak steak; **le steak frites** steak and chips/French fries; **le steak haché** minced beef; **le steak tartare** raw minced beef mixed with a raw egg
le stop* hitch-hiking; **faire du stop*** to hitch-hike
stupide stupid
le stylo pen
le succès success
sucré(e) sweet
le sucre sugar
le sud south
la sueur sweat
suisse Swiss
la Suisse Switzerland
suivre to follow
le sujet subject
super* great, or fantastic; **super-bon*/beau*** really good/good-looking
le super four-star petrol
superbe superb, or beautiful
superficiel(le) superficial
le supermarché supermarket
superstitieux (f: superstitieuse) superstitious
le supplément supplement, or excess fare
supplémentaire extra
supporter to support, or to put up with, or to bear;
je ne supporte pas... I can't stand...
le supporter (football) fan
supposer to suppose
sur on
sûr(e) sure; **bien sûr** of course
le surf (on water) surfing, or (on snow) snowboarding
surfer to surf (sport/Internet)
le surfeur (f: la surfeuse) surfer, or snowboarder
surgelé(e) deep frozen
le surnaturel supernatural
le surnom nickname
la surprise surprise
le/la surveillant(e) de baignade lifeguard
surveiller to watch, or to keep an eye on
le survêtement or **le survêt*** tracksuit
sympathique or **sympa*** friendly, or nice
le syndicat d'initiative tourist office
le synthétiseur or **le synthé*** synthesizer

ta your
le tabac tobacco, or shop where you can buy cigarettes, stamps, phonecards, etc.
la table table
le tableau picture, or board; **le tableau des arrivées/départs** arrivals/departures board
la tache mark, or stain
les tags* [m] graffiti
la taille size, or waist
le tailleur (woman's) suit
se taire to be/keep quiet
le tambour drum or drummer
le tamis sieve
tant pis! too bad!
la tante aunt
taquiner to tease
tard late
taré(e)** crazy, or sick
le tarif price, or rate;
le plein tarif full fare;
le tarif réduit reduced fare
la tarte tart; **la tarte aux pommes** apple pie; **la tarte Tatin** hot caremelized apple pie
la tartelette small tart
la tartine piece of bread spread with butter/jam/pâté, etc.
le tas heap; **un/des tas de** heaps/loads of
la tasse cup
Taureau (star sign) Taurus
le taxi taxi
tchao* bye
la télécabine cable car
la télécommande remote control
le téléphone phone; **le téléphone à carte** card phone; **le téléphone à pièces** coin phone
téléphoner to phone
le télésiège chair lift

le téléski drag lift, or poma© lift
la télévision or **la télé*** television
tellement such, or so
la température temperature
la tempête storm
temporaire temporary
le temps weather, or time; **quel temps fait-il?** what's the weather like? **avoir le temps** to have time; **la mi-temps** half-time; **le temps libre** spare time
les tenailles [f] pliers
tendu(e) tense, or up-tight
tenir to hold
le tennis tennis
la tension blood pressure
tentant(e) tempting
la tente tent
le terrain plot of land, or site, or (sport) pitch, or field
la terrasse terrace
la terre ground, or earth, or land; **par terre** on the ground
terrible terrible, or (slang) out-of-this-world
la tête head; **avoir la tête qui tourne** to feel dizzy; **ça va pas la tête?**** are you crazy?
têtu(e) stubborn
le TGV (train à grande vitesse) very fast train
le thé tea
le théâtre theatre
le thermomètre thermometer
le/la thermos® Thermos® flask
le thon tuna
tiède warm or lukewarm or mild
le/la tien(ne) yours; **à la tienne!** cheers!
les tifs* [m] hair
timbré(e)* mad or crazy
le timbre stamp
timide shy
le tire-au-flanc* skiver
le tire-bouchon corkscrew
le tire-fesses* drag lift
tirer to pull, or to shoot; **tire-toi de là!**** get lost!
la tisane herb tea
le tissu fabric
le titre title, or headline
toi you; **à toi** your turn
les toilettes [f] toilet
le toit roof
la tomate tomato
tomber to fall; **tomber amoureux (f: amoureuse) de** to fall in love with; **tomber en panne** to break down; **tomber sur** to bump into (by chance)
ton your
la tonalité dialling tone
le tonnerre thunder
le top* the best, or the in-thing
le torchon cloth, or tea towel
le tort wrong; **avoir tort** to be wrong
tôt early
la touche key, or button; **avoir/faire une touche*** to make/be a hit (with someone)
toucher to touch
toujours still, or always
la tour tower
le tour turn, or magic trick; **faire un tour** to go for a ride
le tourisme tourism, or sightseeing; **l'office du tourisme [m]** tourist office
le/la touriste tourist
touristique touristy
le tournedos type of steak
la tournée round of drinks, or (music/concert) tour
tourner to turn
le tournevis screwdriver; **le tournevis cruciforme** Phillips© screwdriver
la tourte pie (meat or fish)
tousser to cough
tout(e) all, or everything; **tout à coup** suddenly; **tout à fait** exactly; **tout de suite** immediately; **tout le monde** everybody; **tout le reste** everything else; **tout près** close by; **tout(e) seul(e)** by my/your/him/herself; **tous les autres** everybody else; **tous/toutes les deux** both (of them); **tous les jours** every day
toxique poisonous
le trac: avoir le trac* to have butterflies
traditionnel(le) traditional
la traduction translation
traduire to translate
la tragédie tragedy
le train train
traîner to drag, or to hang around/out
le traitement de texte word processing
le traiteur delicatessen selling ready-made dishes
la tranche slice
tranquille peaceful, or quiet
le transat deck chair
transpirer to sweat
le travail work, or job
travailler to work
travaux (on sign) roadworks
le traveller's chèque traveller's cheque
à travers through
la traversée crossing
traverser to cross, or to go through
très very
la trêve truce
tricher to cheat
le tricot knitting or knitted fabric
le trimestre term
les tripes [f] tripe
triste sad
le trognon (apple) core
le trombone trombone, or paper clip
se tromper to make a mistake
la trompette trumpet
trop too, or too much; **en trop** spare
le trottoir pavement
le trou hole
la trouille: avoir la trouille**** to be/feel scared
la trousse kit, or case; **la trousse à pharmacie** first aid kit
trouver to find
le truc* thing, or tip, or hint
tu you
tuer to kill
le tuba snorkel
le tube* hit song
tuer to kill
les tunes [f]** money, or dosh
la Tunisie Tunisia
le tunnel tunnel
le tuyau pipe, or tip (information)
tuyauter* to give a useful tip
la TVA VAT (value added tax)
le type* bloke, or guy
typique typical

un(e) a, an, or one
unique unique, or the only one; **la fille/le fils unique** only daughter/son
l'université [f] university
l'urgence [f] emergency
urgent(e) urgent
user to wear out
l'usine [f] factory
utile useful

les vacances [f] holiday
les grandes vacances summer holidays/vacation

la vaccination vaccination
vache* mean, or bitchy; **c'est vache*** it's tough/ rotten
la vache cow; **la vache!*** wow!
vachement* very, or really
la vague wave
la vaisselle washing-up
valable valid
la valeur value; **les objets de valeur [m]** valuables
la valise suitcase; **faire les valises** to pack
la vallée valley
la vanille vanilla
se vanter to boast
la varappe rock-climbing
varié(e) varied
le veau veal
la vedette (film/movie) star
végétarien(ne) vegetarian
la veille the day before
le vélo bike; **le vélo de course** racing bike
les vendanges [f] grape harvest
le vendeur (f: la vendeuse) shop assistant
vendre to sell; **à vendre** for sale
vendredi Friday
se venger to get your revenge
venir to come; **venir de (faire quelque chose)** to have just (done something)
le vent wind; **il fait du vent** it's windy
le ventilateur fan
le ventre tummy
le ver worm
le verglas black ice
vérifier to make sure
la vérité truth
le verre glass
vers towards
Verseau (star sign) Aquarius
le versement deposit, or payment
vert(e) green
la veste jacket; **la veste d'équitation** riding jacket; **se prendre une veste** to be beaten hollow; **retourner sa veste** to change sides
le vestiaire changing-room, or cloakroom
les vêtements [m] clothes
vexé(e) offended
la viande meat
vide empty
la vie life; **mener la grande vie** to live it up
vieille (see 'vieux')
Vierge (star sign) Virgo
vieux (f: vieille) old
vif (f: vive) bright, or lively
la vigne vine
le vignoble vineyard
le village village
la ville town, or city
le vin wine
le vinaigre vinegar
la vinaigrette salad dressing made from oil and vinegar
violet(te) purple
le violon violin
le violoncelle cello
le virage bend
virer to turn, or (slang) to fire, or to throw out
la vis screw
le visage face
la visière visor
la visite visit; **rendre visite à** to visit (a person)
visiter to visit (a place)
vite quickly
la vitesse speed, or gear; **à toute vitesse** at full speed
la vitrine (shop) window
vivre to live
v.o.* (version originale) original version (of film/movie)
le vocabulaire vocabulary
le voeu wish
voici here is/are
la voie (railway) track
voilà there is/are
la voile sail, or sailing; **la grand-voile** main sail
le voilier sailing boat
voir to see
le/la voisin(e) neighbour
la voiture car**la voix** voice
le vol flight, or theft
la volaille poultry
le volant steering wheel
voler to fly, or to steal
le volet shutter
le voleur (f: la voleuse) thief
le volley(-ball) volleyball
vomir to be sick (vomit)
le vote vote
votre your
le/la vôtre yours; **à la vôtre!** cheers!
vouloir (see p.45) to want; **vouloir dire** to mean
vous you (see also p. 44)
le voyage journey, or trip; **le voyage organisé** package tour; **bon voyage!** have a good trip!
voyager to travel
le voyageur (f: la voyageuse) traveller
le voyou thug
vrai(e) true
vraiment really
le VTT (vélo tout terrain) mountain bike
la vue view, or sight

le wagon wagon, or (train) carriage; **le wagon restaurant** restaurant car; **le wagon-lit** sleeping car
les WC [m] loo,or toilet
le week-end weekend

le yaourt yogurt
les yeux [m] eyes

zéro zero
le zoo zoo
le zoom zoom lens

This edition first published in 2009 by Usborne Publishing Ltd., Usborne House, 83-85 Saffron Hill, London EC1N 8RT, England. www.usborne.com

Printed in Dubai, UAE.